Orlando Gough

# Coming & Going

*Uniformbooks*

First published 2021
Copyright © Orlando Gough
ISBN 978–1–910010–27–3

*Uniformbooks*
7 Hillhead Terrace, Axminster, Devon EX13 5JL
uniformbooks.co.uk

Trade distribution in the UK by Central Books
centralbooks.com

Printed and bound by T J Books, Padstow, Cornwall

*to Jo*
*to Daniel and Milo*
*to Piers and Jamie*

# Salt

# Gull

# Queer

# Angel

—

It is the day of my funeral. Jo has her instructions. She never wanted this but I insisted.

Dusk. A small crowd gathers on the beach near the West Pier. Dogs and wolves wander through the crowd, and through the water. There is an offshore breeze. A brass band plays a medley of Fatboy Slim hits. Daniel and Milo launch a wooden sailing boat that Daniel has made. My body lies in a wicker coffin on the deck. Milo makes a teasing speech.

The breeze takes the boat out from the shore. The crowd watches silently, excited, anxious. The band plays a massively slowed-down sea shanty. A flock of swifts on a vesper flight rises high in the air, higher and higher, disappears from sight.

As the music comes to a climax, the boat bursts into flames. The crowd gasps. Some people cheer, some clap, others are profoundly disturbed. Jo is beyond comfort.

A minute or two later the music is drowned out by the frenzied sound of sirens. The police and the fire department and the ambulances screech on to the promenade. And soon after, members of the Brighton and Hove Health and Safety Executive.

—

I was born here (in a town), I live here now (in a city). A city that is a seaside resort. A seaside resort that is a city. A city that has a reputation for tolerance, for permissiveness, for scuzziness, for petty crime, for shingle, for improving your health, for ruining your health. It's a city where you can be a freak and not feel like a freak.

—

I spend my entire childhood at school, continuously. My father teaches at Brighton College, a private boys' school in Kemp Town. He is a House Master—he looks after sixty boys who live together in a house, and copy each other's homework. We live next door, in a flat whose balcony is directly above the school kitchen. I learn, from my brother Jamie, about guerrilla cookery, poking snails and earth and weeds through the air conditioning vents into the custard. I learn how to climb trees, how to reflect sunlight into my father's classroom, how to ride a bike with no brakes, how to provoke the Head Master, whose power over us is limited. I go to different schools, schools far away, to be taught, and return to Brighton College for my holidays, to the oppressive flint buildings, to the smell of lemon verbena, to my rhubarb patch, to my parents. At the beginning of each holiday I have to get to know them again.

—

I am walking home with my father, up Edward Street, up Eastern Road. Unfortunately the street is lined with junk shops. We stop in every one. He looks, he exclaims, he leaves. He looks, he exclaims, he puts in an offer. He is profoundly happy.

—

My mother has two jobs, only one of which is paid. Her fulfilling paid job is as an interior designer. She designs furniture, fabrics, blinds, in a style influenced by the interiors of the Royal Pavilion. Her favourite material is bamboo. Her other, time-consuming, infuriating unpaid job is as a slave of Brighton College, looking after the wellbeing of the boys in my father's house, dealing with the employees, being at my father's side when he needs her. She never complains—or rather she never complains in front of us children. But then, that is how my parents behave: they never argue in front of us, there is never any strife in front of us, everything we witness is harmonious.

—

My brothers and I spend hours in Kemp Town Station, derelict, disused, out of bounds, irresistible. We occasionally steal a sign—GENTLEMEN, COLMANS MUSTARD, KEEP OFF THE TRACK. Leading away from the station is a tunnel, an alluring tunnel that leads under the hill to the Lewes Road, an unimaginably long tunnel. DANGER—FALLING MASONRY—KEEP OUT. We will walk through the tunnel we will show each other our bravery we will miraculously reach the other end a different world we will be heroes.

We walk into the tunnel, hopping between the sleepers. The light begins to go. We have no torch. We are alarmed. The light goes. We are terrified. We dash back to the light at the end of the.

—

Here we are in St Bartholomew's Church, built on the dimensions of Noah's Ark (ready for the next Flood?). There are no cabins. Just one vast space. The biggest room in the universe. I'm ten years old. My parents have brought us here for a three-hour service on Good Friday. I'm in the most extreme realms of boredom, feeling sick from the incense that is whirled about, and I'm begging for mercy (not from God, from my parents). Ssssh. It'll be over soon. (Really?) It's good for you. (Really?) Listen. The sounds of the voices rise up, become liquid, swirl around over our heads. Listening to them is like drowning. We are at the bottom of the sea. I am casting around for something to focus on, and find myself fixating on the altars. Shiny, kitsch, ornate, militantly high-church, they look like jukeboxes. Put a coin in and… maybe that's what we're listening to.

—

I am under water in the Brighton College swimming pool (which is also a theatre, my father directs plays in here… how can that be?). I'm in the shallow end, which is deep. I'm in a panic. I am going to drown, I am going to drown, I am going to… A strange animal, a whale with long hair billowing out, looms towards me, pulls me out of the water. It is my mother. What an all-round service—she gives me life, she saves my life.

—

My father is trying to teach me to swim. It's not going well. The water, cold, grey, fierce, pulls at my legs. I can hardly stand up. I don't want to launch myself. Behind us, a wall of pebbles.

The beach is so steep here that we can't see the town. We're on our own. My father waits patiently, but I can see that he's frustrated.

Where is Martha Gunn?

—

It's a summer day, calm seas, auspicious gales, a shoal of swimmers, a flotilla of paddleboards, disturbed only by the occasional speedboat. 180° of blue, 180° of freedom. But where is the natural harbour? Where is the river? Where are the islands? The relationship of land and sea is too simple.

—

Beyond, the wind farm. A far-sighted, graceful source of energy | an eyesore, a bird killer, a shipping hazard, a waste of tax-payers' money. The blades turn, gently, gently. Time moves slowly here. At night the warning lights dance in unison:
dp and dah two three and dah two three and and and
dp and dah two three and dah two three and and and
dp and dah two three and dah two three and and and

Beyond, oil tankers on the horizon (defiant messages to the wind farm). If you watch intently for five minutes you can detect that they are moving.

—

And beyond the horizon, France. It's there, you just have to believe. Françoise Hardy, the croissant, Napoleon, but but Degas, Jeanne Moreau, Olivier Messiaen and and sex and let them eat cake but Genet Camus Sartre 1968. It's there! You can swim there (can you? from Brighton?). You can certainly sail there. Which Johnny Franklin and I do and we float lazily into Le Havre, and on the way back there is scarcely any wind and the atmosphere is heavy and we are scarcely moving and gradually the wind starts to get up up up and halfway across we are hit by a storm did we look at the weather forecast why are we doing this god knows, in need of artificial adventure, that must be it, activities which were once practical, productive are now a matter of choice, a way of giving our lives a fillip, what was once work is now leisure, we can choose to test ourselves against the sea and so let's test ourselves, the sea rages and the waves smash into the bow of the boat, cascade over the stern, we are being attacked from in front and behind, it's like being in a boxing ring with twenty opponents and I am terrified, useless, and Johnny is terrified, capable, reefing in the sails, riding the waves, as I cower and contemplate the fact that at a time when he most needs my help I have no help to give, this could go either way, this could go either way, and LOOK there is a line of cliffs and there is Brighton Marina and here we are in the harbour, out of breath, and the wind drops completely, how come? and we're bobbing about in the water, becalmed, and we can breathe, we've made it back, achievement, relief, escape, and then there is an enormous gust of wind and the yacht is smashed into the sea wall.

—

It's a winter day, sunset. The starlings, from Ditchling, from Brighton, from Scandinavia, gather to roost on the West Pier. One starling takes off and ten thousand starlings (really? who says? well, count them) follow. The reaction time is a fraction of a second. The world's best screensaver, but it's live. The world's best formation dancing team, but it's three-dimensional. They fly with each other, through each other, round each other, in a shape-shifting bubble.

—

The west wind blows, and the beach moves. Longshore drift! There are a thousand attempts to control this movement— groynes made of wood, of concrete, of flints, of iron, of steel, that lie sleeping in the beach, stretching out into the sea.

—

The bandstand—it's a pagoda, it's a birdcage on top of a café. A beautiful wrought-iron cage, a benevolent cage, a cage from which escape is possible. Except for the sound of a brass band, which seems imprisoned, unable to escape, drowned out by the sea and the wind and the traffic.

—

It's a summer day, sunset. The sky is blue, but there is a cloud of smoke over the beach. It looks as if there is a massive funeral rite in progress. We might be on the banks of the Ganges. In fact it is many small funeral rites, for many cows. There is a ferocious smell of barbecuing burgers, and paraffin.

—

Michael sits in a shelter on the beach promenade, playing the clarinet, always in the same shelter. His playing is wayward, distracted. He has seven or eight tunes (yes, including *Stranger on the Shore*), and he jumps from one to another, loses his thread, leaves off at random, stares out to sea, takes the instrument apart, puts it back together, plays again.

—

I'm walking down our street towards the beach. The west wind blows. There are three layers of sound—off-white noise: the turbulent sea, the wind as it climbs round the contours of the Holiday Inn Hotel (Charles Dickens, says the plaque, was a frequent visitor), the traffic. Despite spending most of my life as a musician, I can't tell the difference.

—

Listen.
The seagull mews, squawks, squeaks, growls, yelps, laughs, groans, sings.
It flies *yeeow* anxious, plaintive.
It sits on a knackered wrought iron gantry of the West Pier *kek-kek kek-kek*.
It flies keeow under threat *keeeeooooow* under threat *keeeeeeeooooooow*.
*Keeow-keeow-keeow-gah-gah-gah*.
It fights over territory *huoh-huoh-huoh*.
It rips into a bin bag.
It sits on a lamp post *kek-kek kek-kek*.
It eats fish and chips.
It flirts *huoh-huoh-huoh*.
It refuses to move *huoh-huoh-huoh*.

It eats a dead rabbit.

It forages at night in West Street. It eats some vomit.

It sees a predator *ha-ha-ha-ha*.

It flirts *klee-ew klee-ew*.

It fucks *kwa-kwa-kwa*.

It makes a nest on the roof of our house.

*Keeoch-keeoch-keeoch*, it sings. *Kree-ah, kuk-kuk-kuk, kwaaarr kwaaarr, kwup-kwup-kwup.*

Listen.

—

"What are those brightly coloured boxes?"

"They're beach huts. Aren't they lovely?"

"But they're not on the beach. The beach is over there. They're on this... runway."

"It's a, it's a walkway. It's called a promenade."

"But look at those people. They're running."

"They're trying to keep fit. Or maybe they're trying to get fit."

"I want a hut. We could live in there."

"Well, it's a bit small. And there's no running water."

"So... we could keep chickens in there. A hutch! A beach hutch!"

"I don't think the chickens'd be very happy."

"They could run around all over the beach."

"Could they?"

"And they could swim in the sea. Can chickens swim?"

"Er..."

"And they could fly to Worthing, and then they could come back to their hut."

"I..."

"*Please*, let's get a hut."

"I don't think we could afford one."

"*Please*. You said they were lovely. What do other people keep in their huts? Do they keep chickens?"

"They keep chairs I think. They put the chairs outside the hut and sit on them. And they keep a kettle."

"What do they want a kettle for?"

"So they can make tea."

"But they don't have any water."

—

I set off westwards, into the west wind, past beach huts, and more beach huts.

Here is a row of large lumpy expensive white houses, occupied (spasmodically) by bankers and likeable TV stars, and here in front of them is an outrage (a very unusual outrage on this part of the coast): a stretch of private beach. So this must be the South Coast Riviera. Surely the beach should be covered with sun loungers and umbrellas? No, it's empty, and it's never used. Strange, the houses seem to have no access to the beach. Perhaps the expensive residents are afraid.

—

Beyond is the port, a (natural!) harbour, the nearest Brighton gets to being industrial (and it's not Brighton, it's Hove, no, it's Portslade and Southwick and Shoreham). (Brighton industry? Typewriters (once upon a time), bubble cars (once upon a time), video games, skunk.) It's a place for landing timber, steel, fish, a place of fierce fences and ferocious signage. The seaward spit of land is a threshold between industry and the sea—a beach where many of the groynes, wood and steel, have been so eroded by salt water and wind that they no longer have any practical purpose. They are works of art. (One of Brighton's most prolific artists—the sea!) Here is a random iron post, covered with rust, with a massive colony of mussels clinging to it. On the beach are dog walkers, and anglers searching for worms, and naked men, and sometimes the dogs show an interest in the worms, and sometimes in the naked men. And here is a group of Nigerian men in white robes, praying for the gay men and the naked men of Brighton to be saved. They sing and their bodies sway, and as the tide comes in they move gracefully up the beach, towards the sea wall on which someone has written "I really dislike paella". And here at the end of the beach, near the harbour mouth, is a café which used to be called Carrots until the new management took it instantaneously upmarket not by changing the menu but by renaming it Carats.

—

Today the beach is covered with timber. The shipwrecked boat is miles away up the coast, but the contents is here. Timber everywhere, piles of timber, spilling over the groynes. It is an offence to remove wood from this beach! But it's ours isn't it? We could build a new town, a wooden town.

—

On the bandstand, there is a pre-nup photoshoot. Vikram and Rob are having their photos taken by a professional photographer whose bossiness is uniting them in irritation. A bullfinch sits on the balustrade, singing.

—

The i360 goes up and down, up and down. ("A vertical pier"— clever sales pitch.) The shiniest object in Brighton. We take a ride. (A "flight", it's called. Ah, now that would be exciting. The pod rises up the spindle, spins round, faster and faster, up, up, takes off at the top, flies stomach-churningly above the city, lands, splash, in the sea, emergency procedures.)

We look down and see the city. There's our house! We look down and see the sea. To say the sea is blue—that won't do —it's a thousand shades of blue, and these blue blues have a thousand textures. "The blueness of the blue went through my eye into my very being", wrote William Beebe after being at the depths of the ocean in his Bathysphere. It's a feeling I have as I look down from the i360. But (like Beebe) we're indoors! Where's the sound? Where's the sea air?

—

This is our house. A wrought iron verandah wraps round the bay on the façade. Very Brighton. Very sugar plantation.

—

This is our house. And this is our garden. Oh no, it's not a garden, it's a small terrace. It wasn't always this small. Sometime in the 1920s the owner of the house next door wins three-quarters of our garden at backgammon (backgammon?

poker? let's say backgammon), and three-quarters of the three gardens on the other side. Not half, three-quarters. Oof. He also wins the bathroom at the top of our house. (It has since been returned, but the outline of the connecting doorway is still visible.) So the next-door garden is massive, T-shaped. The backgammon expert—can you be a backgammon expert? surely it's mainly luck?—parades his success, has a tennis court built. Tok tok, tok tok. Infuriating. (The court has gone. Our neighbour Shan raises plants in a greenhouse, grows tropical palms and exotic flowers, cultivates a vegetable patch which we share. Big society!)

—

I'm walking up our street towards the shops. Eddie is at the corner, as usual. We meet several times every day.
"Would you like an apple?" he says. His voice is parched, cracked, like a dried-up river bed.
"No thanks."
"What's your name?"
"Orlando."
"No it's not. What is it?"
"It's Orlando."
"I don't believe you. What is it?"
"It's Orlando, really."
"You're lying. I don't want to talk to you. You're a liar. Would you like an apple?"

—

The man is wearing only boxer shorts. He is bound to the lamp post by a roll of cling film. His body is smeared with flour and egg. Across the road, in the open window of a bar, his friends his friends the men in his life the ones he holds dear are taunting him. A light rain begins to fall. The flour and egg mixture is turning to glue.
"Are you ok?" we say.
"I'm fine", he says.
"Would you like us to release you?" we say.
"Oh no", he says.
"Is she worth it?" we say.

"Oh yes", he says, "she's wonderful. She's worth it."
"She's worth it, she's worth it, she's worth it", sing the men
in his life,
"In wind and in rain she's worth all the pain,
She's worth it, she's worth it, she's worth it."
No they don't. They sing:
"She's a fat slag
All she needs is a shag."

—

The café is busy, raucous. But Symon is silent. He comes in
every day, alone, at exactly 11am, drinks a cup of espresso and
a glass of iced water. (He used to smoke a cigar.) In 1940, as a
child, he escaped from Lviv and came to live here. Marek, who
serves him, arrived in Brighton from Poland three weeks ago,
illegally. He is due to be deported next week.

Outside the café is a sign: If you voted for Brexit, don't bother
to come in.

—

Vikram and Rob are being married in the music room of the
Pavilion. "My great-great-grandfather was here", says Vikram,
"in this room, in 1914, recovering from his injuries at Ypres.
Apparently he was quite a hero."

—

Wartz is everywhere.
Wartz Wartz Wartz.
And the war on Wartz.
Wartz, whose tag is on this council refuse bin, is an estate
agent.
Wartz, whose tag is on the wall of this estate agent's, is a
twelve-year old girl whose parents have split up but who still
love each other.
Wartz, who is the brand manager for the Wartz brand, is an
artist disillusioned with conventional techniques.
Wartz, who understands that the most important thing in life,
more important than family, more important than wealth,

more important than love, is a recognisable identity.

Wartz, who understands that the letter Z is an essential component of a successful brand name.

Wartz, whose tag is on this chimney of the Royal Pavilion, is a council worker demoralised by his stupid pointless job.

Wartz, whose tag is on the railway viaduct over the London Road, is a gymnast disillusioned by her sexist treatment in the world of gymnastics.

The war on Wartz is mostly in the hands of Sisyphus, a council worker. Sisyphus is armed only with an endless supply of grey paint, and that's not enough. He can't keep up with Wartz. And the grey paint, the grey paint is an invitation.

Wartz, whose tag is, since yesterday, on our front wall, lives in our area, we think.

Now we are involved in the war on Wartz. We are watching, watching.

We have enlisted our neighbours on WartzWatch, but no one has reported any sightings. Still the tags keep appearing.

—

There is a rumour that the council has introduced farm animals into the city as a traffic-calming initiative. I cycle experimentally down Kings Road, on the seafront. No farm animals in sight, but I am nearly run down by a boy racer.

—

I am making Flummery from the Martha Gunn Recipe Book. An angel at my table. "To a quart of fine ground oatmeal put three quarts of water which you must pour of once, in twelve hours for three times. You must pour it on very clear and the third time you must straine it and boyle it till tis thick enough."

I'm off round the corner to buy oatmeal at Taj, a shop that sells five different kinds of oatmeal and fifteen different kinds of freekeh. (I know, overkill, but.) Almost all the assistants are East European. In the early mornings the musak (that can't be the right word) is sung sections of the Q'ran. I like to go in at this time. Later it becomes South Asian pop music. I like to go in then too.

"I haven't been to Brighton recently", says Nick Tigg. "Is it still full of brightly-coloured crap?" Later that afternoon I'm in Blackout, buying gorgeous Mexican brightly-coloured crap, made out of tin. Blackout is in the North Laine, a grid of modest streets of modest Victorian terraced houses, which you could argue is the main attraction of Brighton for visitors, since it has been colonised by shops selling gorgeous brightly-coloured crap that no one needs. This is not a butchers!

—

I walk past Tattooing at Gunpoint. We are Hove's longest running custom tattooist. We have one mission: to bring creativity and artistic quality to the tattooing scene. No pain, no grrr, says Scrow. Introductory offer.

No, don't tattoo me, please don't! That's not what I want! That's not what I want at all! I don't want ink under my skin! Please! Please! Please!

(Yes, I was born here, but should I be living here? I'm a lousy swimmer, I'm not gay, gay, gay, and I don't want a tattoo.)

—

Daniel (I have a son!) is working the night shift at a mini-market in Kemp Town. Alcohol is king, violence is always a possibility. The owner of the shop sits upstairs watching the CCTV on two giant screens, smoking dope and taking the occasional line of cocaine. If there is any trouble in the shop, she comes down and headbutts the offenders. Peak time is 3am when the clubs close. But the pub next door is open all night. Men men men emerge—otters, foxes, bears, drag artists—flirt with Daniel and dive back in again.

—

This is Black Rock. Stranded between the city and the marina. A lost space. Once there was an Art Deco lido here, then a derelict Art Deco lido. Now there is nothing. But it's a useful space, a space for gay men to have outdoor sex, protected from the public gaze by the lush landscape of Duke's Mound, a space for raves, a space for not doing the right thing. Tonight: Bob Dobbs and the Church of the SubGenius, a mockcult that parodies Scientology, organises raves and puts up candidates in general elections. The advance publicity is subtle: tiny flyers appear on lampposts, headshots of a preppy-looking man smoking a pipe; but everyone who needs to know knows what they mean.

—

There is a rumour that yesterday evening at dusk a neighbourhood of Whitehawk, a sprawling hilly suburb that struggles with poverty, disappeared for several hours—a housing estate, a primary school, an industrial park. In its place there was a vast meadow. According to the rumour several beautiful grey Palomino horses were grazing. This morning the neighbourhood appears entirely back to normal. ("Back to normal"? So we believe the rumour?)

—

I am walking through the city.
I walk on tarmac, on paving stones, on wood, on concrete, on cobbles.
This synagogue is not just a synagogue, it's a yoga studio.
This mosque is in a detached suburban house.
This industrial space is now a gym. Exercise was work; now it is leisure.
This housing estate is next to a Neolithic camp.
These two elm trees, twins, were planted four hundred years ago. Soon there will only be one. Dutch Elm Disease has, finally, arrived in Brighton.
This gasometer is still here! What to do with it?
This cabaret club used to be a mausoleum, a replica of the mausoleum in the courtyard of a synagogue in India.
In this gallery, converted from a riding school, there is an exhibition of paintings made in Brighton two hundred years ago.
This restaurant, an imitation of a Parisian brasserie, is in a former Methodist chapel.

This pawnbrokers used to be a House of Correction.

In this concert hall, converted from riding stables, a symphony is being played which Beethoven wrote in the year the riding stables were completed.

In this cinema, the oldest cinema in Britain, a film set in the 1960s of a book set in Brighton in the 1930s is being shown.

In this area, there have been buildings for seven hundred years. There is a palpable sense of the city as it was then, its industry, its trade, its social interactions. But actually all those buildings have been replaced. Nothing remains but parts of the layout. Shadows.

—

```
        N O R T H   S T R E E T
   W                           E
   E                           A
   S                           S
   T                           T

   S                           S
   T                           T
   R                           R
   E                           E
   E                           E
   T                           T
        S O U T H   S T R E E T
```

They knew how to name streets in medieval Brighton. West Street, North Street, East Street, South Street, all where they should be. Middle Street in the middle (roughly). Ship Street where you dream of maritime adventures. Black Lion Street, where you dream of adventures on the edge of possibility. Quadrophrenia Alley, where... no, not yet.

For several centuries West Street, North Street, East Street and South Street define the boundaries of the town. Beyond are sheep and mackerel. Inside are The Lanes, narrow, claustrophobic, smelly.

A group of women, Minnie Turner, Barbara Hulanicki, Zoella, Ellen Nye Chart, Vesta Tilley, Elizabeth Robins, Esther Downes, Mary Shelley, Caroline Lucas, Anna Maria Crouch, Gertrude Perks, Octavia Wilberforce moves through the Lanes, past a hundred jewellery shops, singing Dusty Springfield's *I Only Want To Be With You*, a cappella. (Who do they only want to be with? (Oh, come on, it's just a song.)) Not far from them, a group of men, Edward Carpenter, Gioachino Rossini, Patrick Hamilton, Nick Cave, Jack Buchanan, Harry Cowley, Pinkie Brown, Laurence Olivier, Mohandas Gandhi, Max Miller, Henry Salt, C. B. Fry, David Walliams, are grouped in Little East Street, singing *There's Always Something There To Remind Me*, while Le Gateau Chocolat and Douglas Byng, both dressed as Dusty, in miniskirts, with bouffant blond hair, panda eye makeup, pretend to go through a marriage ceremony on one of the balconies of the Town Hall. The two groups will maraud round the Lanes all evening, through medieval streets, through twittens, through shopping precincts. They will never meet —they don't need to. They are each, for the moment, happy together.

(A twitten? Sorry. A narrow lane, an alleyway, a place for escaping, for hiding, for having sex, for short cuts, for drug deals.)

Wait a minute. Where's South Street? It's not where it should be. It's moved from its place in the perfect geometry, washed away several hundred years ago. Now it's a back street, not a back street in the sense of not being a main street, a back street which is the back of the city. If you turned the city inside out, it would be South Street (and Farm Yard (yes, really, Farm Yard (no traffic-calming sheep here)), and Little Preston Street). A street of bins, of air conditioning units, of graffiti, of back doors, of fire escapes. Keep clear. CCTV cameras in operation. Crew only. The bins have a message: Do not climb into or sleep in this bin. This could result in serious injury or death.

Does anyone ever walk down here? Oh yes, here are the remains of a battered fish. Edie is excited.

—

Mackerel
(in 1600 fishing is *the* Brighton industry)
(drawnett shotnett tucknett harbour cok flew)
(mackerel plaice conger herring)
(mackerel is *the* catch)
(beware of storms!)
(The sea is very unkind, writes Daniel Defoe,
and the inhabitants might reasonably expect
it would eat up the whole town)

becomes

fish and chips
(here we are by the sea)
(but you can't batter a mackerel)
(yes but where does that cod come from?)

becomes

vegetarian fish and chips
(pioneered by Terre à Terre in East Street)
(halloumi = fish)
(but we're not in the Levant)
(yes but this is "Better Batter:
soft buttermilk soaked halloumi,
dipped in chip shop batter,
served with vodka-spiked preserve plum tomatoes,
bright fresh pea hash with pickled quails egg,
sea salad tartar and chubby chips,
finished with lemony Yemeni relish")
(we're close to where the fish used to be landed,
but we don't need fish)

becomes, eventually

vegan fish and chips
(how do you do that?)

It's a family thing—Jo, me, Daniel, Milo. We are in St Nicholas
Rest Garden to bury Caspar. The Rest Garden is a small
cemetery, part of the graveyard of the Church of St Nicholas
of Myra (strapline: The Ancient Mother Church of Brighton).
There are simple gravestones all round the perimeter, a terrace
of burial vaults, and a few elaborate monuments in the central
area. Most of the stones are so old that the engraving has
completely eroded; they have become anonymous memorials.
It's late evening, dark. We're not the only ones in the garden.
There are people walking their dogs, and people doing drug
deals.

We search around for a suitable spot for Caspar. Caspar is—
was—a bearded dragon, a lizard-like reptile that normally
lives in the Australian desert. He, no, she, no, he—we never
discovered his, no, her sex—was unlucky enough to find his
way into a pet shop in Brighton, and then even more unlucky
to find her way into a heated vivarium in Daniel's bedroom,
where he lived a sad, lonely, impotent life, a shadow of the
life she might have led in Australia. He became disgustingly
obese, her body spreading out till he looked like a CD on legs.
Her death seemed to Jo and me a merciful release—for us
(guilty to have been complicit in his imprisonment) and her.

We find a spot, and start to dig. Daniel cries a little. How do
you have an emotional relationship with a bearded dragon?
A lurcher comes over to sniff the grave. Nearby a woman
prepares crack cocaine.

As we leave, we pass a man in a hoodie and tartan trousers
curled up asleep on a monument to Sir Richard Phillips, Knight,
born in 1767, a publisher, "a scoundrel who would suck the
knowledge out of authors' skulls and fling the carcasses on
the dunghill", an ardent supporter of Thomas Paine, a prison
reformer, "one of the most accomplished rogues in his majes-
ties domain", a vegetarian, an educationalist, a man who has
disproved, he claims, Newton's Theory of Gravity (apples fall
upwards!), Sheriff of London (despite having been imprisoned

for distributing copies of Paine's *Rights of Man*), a man who goes bankrupt, avoids the debtors' prison, and manages to keep his businesses alive.

His epitaph, which he has written himself, pays tribute to his perfect life. "He lived through an age of memorable events and changes and was an active and anxious contemporary something" (redacted by time) "and an effective ameliorator of a stern and uncharitable criminal code and the inventor and promulgator of the Interrogative System of Education" (radical idea, don't just lecture, ask questions) "by which new impulses were given to the intelligence of society and something something developed the laws of nature on immutable principles and wrote and published more original works than any of his contemporaries and in all of them advocated Civil Liberty, General something or other, Ascendancy of Justice and the improvement of the Human Race; and as a husband, father and friend was an example for imitation leaving a mourning family little to inherit besides this good name he died in the enjoyment of that peace which the sweet truth of the Christian Religion and the world can never give nor take away."

We walk home, dragonless, past Martha Gunn, underground, past Phoebe Hessel, past Anna Maria Crouch, past Sake Dean Mahomet. Angels of the area.

–

Brighton begins to become its present self in about 1760— hang on, surely Brighton begins to become its present self as soon as it exists (ageing starts at birth!)—well, ok, ok, but in about 1760 it veers abruptly towards its present self: it becomes a resort. The new bourgeoisie wants to travel, not for work but for leisure—the first stirrings of tourism!—and for Londoners the nearest convenient seaside spot is Brighton. The sea is still useful for extracting mackerel from, but now it's more useful for bathing. The bathing is not simply for pleasure—it's for health. Aaaaah, self-improvement allied to pleasure—no need for guilt. And if you want to be well, don't just bathe in the seawater, drink it, says Doctor Richard Russell to the patients who come to his glamorous surgery on the seafront. Rub your body with seaweed. "The sea washes away the ills of men", he says, quoting from Euripides.

Here in Brighton (scandal!) the bathing is mixed—women and men together, no barriers. But there is some privacy, provided by the dippers.

Martha Gunn is the Queen of the Dippers, the Venerable Priestess of the Bath. For anxious bathers, the way it works is this: the bathing machine, a wooden hut on wheels, is pulled out into the sea, by people, by horses. The anxious bather is helped into the sea by conscientious helpful strong active careful bathing assistants, dippers, "in every aspect adapted to their employment", taken care of, protected from prying eyes, protected from the possibility of drowning in choppy waters, and returned to shore in the machine. What a service!

—

Boy George, Prince of Wales, comes to Brighton for the first time in 1783. He likes racing and gambling, hunting, dining and dancing, music and theatre. He is ill. He has always been ill. The sea air will help his gout. Perhaps he will drink some seawater. He is accompanied by his lover, Maria Fitzherbert, already twice widowed. He is infatuated by her. They get married, secretly, in the drawing-room of her house, knowing that the marriage is illegal—it has not had the approval of the king and the Privy Council.

Brighton grows. It becomes "London-by-the-sea". "When I tell you that fifty-two public coaches go from hence to London every day and bring people down for six shillings", says Maria, "you will not be surprised at the sort of company we have".

But this is not London! London doesn't have Martha Gunn.

Britain expands its empire, goes to war with France, trades in slaves, grows rich.

Martha Gunn becomes indispensable to Boy George and Maria. "To Brighton came he", sing the dippers, "Came George III's son, To be bathed in the sea By famed Martha Gunn." She is allowed into the inner sanctum of the Pavilion, the kitchen. She is a national treasure. In the frisky 1794 print *French Invasion or Brighton in a Bustle* by John Colley Nixon, French troops invade Brighton. (Too near France! A dangerous place to be. (In 1514, during some war or other, a posse of French soldiers has hopped over the Channel and burnt the entire town to the ground.)) The Battle of Brighton Beach. The French troops are repelled by Martha Gunn and two other brave dippers. Martha lifts an invading officer off the ground with one hand while she prepares to punch him with the other. Under her feet is a pile of Frenchmen, vanquished.

In 1795 George is introduced to Caroline of Brunswick. He is disturbed by the sight of her. She is unattractive and unhygienic, he thinks. He orders brandy. She is disturbed by the sight of him. "He is very fat", she says, "and he is nothing like as handsome as his portrait." He marries her. The marriage is, er, essential—his debts are paid off. Next year, Caroline gives birth to a daughter. Three days later George writes his will, leaving all his "worldly property... to my Maria Fitzherbert, my wife, the wife of my heart and soul".

George commissions a massive stable block and riding house, far larger than his villa. As the domed roof, based on the one at the Paris Corn Exchange, is being built, there is a fear that it will collapse once the scaffolding has been removed. But the doomsters and gloomsters are wrong. "The cupola is now on", writes the architect William Porden, "and the workmen are swarming about it like jackdaws. The whole proves fully equal to expectation. The dome now supports itself, without the assistance of scaffolding, and has not yet fallen."

In 1811 George has been heir to the throne for forty-nine years. He becomes Prince Regent, the acting monarch. Maria has become an embarrassment, as she is a Catholic; so she is dismissed. Later he says that whenever he mentions her name "it is with feelings of disgust and horror", that their marriage was "artificial, just to satisfy her".

His father is mentally ill. The king's main interest is teaching bullfinches to sing, using a miniature mechanical organ that plays eight tunes.

*Eight Songs For A Mad King* is a music theatre piece for singer and small ensemble by Peter Maxwell Davies, written in 1969. The songs are the king's monologue as he listens to his birds perform. His voice is ravaged, rendered almost inhuman by day-long soliloquies. The first performance is sung by Roy Hart. He has a five-octave range (most people have two or less) and can sing chords, a technique that he has been taught by the Jewish German Alfred Wolfsohn. Wolfsohn, having served as a stretcher bearer in World War I, had suffered auditory hallucinations of screaming soldiers whom he had witnessed dying. He was diagnosed with shell shock. He had cured himself by vocalising the extreme sounds he had heard.

The piece takes the mechanical organ's tunes, and other contemporary tunes, from the *Messiah* and elsewhere, fragments them, distorts them, layers them in surreal ways. The musicians play from inside giant birdcages. They represent the bullfinches. (The percussionist represents the king's keeper.) One of the movements is written on staves shaped like a birdcage. At the climax of the piece, in the seventh song, the king reaches into the violinist's cage, grabs the violin and smashes it—the killing of a bullfinch, and the moment of surrender to his insanity. In the eighth, he announces his own death.

Meanwhile Boy George is in charge of the country. He wants to party. Brighton is the place. He commissions the architect John Nash to expand his villa into a pleasure palace. The Pavilion is a confusion | a brilliant synthesis of Indian and Islamic styles. A stately pleasure-dome. Two hundred years of colonialism and foreign trade, two hundred years of East India Company rule have given architects and their patrons ideas. Ruthless cultural appropriation | a respectful, loving tribute. Domes, towers, cupolas, minarets. The pavilion has a dreamlike quality, light, temporary, like a fantastic tent. "It is a whim", says the Austrian statesman Klemens von Metternich. "It is a madhouse", says the Comtesse de Boigne.

—

The site just across the Old Steine from the Pavilion is up for development. My brother Piers is asked to put forward a scheme. I am not, partly I'm guessing because I am not an architect. But I have a scheme, the only architectural idea I have ever had. It is a scheme that must be realised, a scheme that will bring Agra to Brighton: a replica of the Pavilion in black marble. (On the ground floor will be a branch of Taj.) "It is a whim", says Klemens von Metternich. "I know", I say.

Piers designs a block of flats, because he has to, a frisky block of flats. Neither of our schemes is built. Failure of imagination.

—

The inside of the Pavilion, decorated by Frederick Crace and Robert Jones, is Neo-ClassicalChineseGothicMoghul. Porcelain pagodas decorated with dragons, dolphins and dogs. Lotus-shaped chandeliers. Silk and lacquerware imported from China and Japan. Strange hybrid objects are commissioned —an English organ decorated with Chinese motifs.

Concerts, balls, banquets.

One of the most beautiful rooms is the plainest: the kitchen. Palm leaves emerge magically from the top of thin iron pillars. The range is magnificent, technologically advanced. The kitchen is an important room, since George loves food; and pioneeringly, it is next to the dining room, so hot food is possible. George employs the great French chef Marie-Antoine Carême to cook a banquet. Carême creates a three-act grand opera of dishes—one: soups, hors d'oeuvres, entrées, relevés; two: roasts, fishes, entremets; three: desserts. Carême's speciality is pâtisserie. "The fine arts", he says, "are five in number, to wit: painting, sculpture, poetry, music, architecture—whose main branch is confectionery." The Pavilion is constructed out of pastry, a Turkish mosque entirely from marzipan. Here are the ruins of Antioch. Here is a Syrian hermitage and here is a Chinese hermitage. And here is Carême's signature dish: *croquembouche*, a mass of profiteroles, filled with cream, piled into a cone and bound together with spun sugar. George says, "It is wonderful to be back in Brighton where I am truly loved."

After the banquet, Carême and Martha Gunn sit in the kitchen, picking at the leftovers. A small fraction of the food has been eaten. The rest is being divided amongst the cooks and the waiters.

"These spoilt fuckers", says Carême, "I could serve them rats and they wouldn't know the difference."

"Try it", says Martha Gunn. "By the way, don't you think this way of serving everything at once is a bit disgusting? It's a dog's dinner. Why don't you bring in the dishes one at a time, when they are hot and fresh?"

"You don't understand. It's about display, it's about theatre", says Carême.

"Then stop complaining", says Martha Gunn.

The music room is an important room, since George loves music. (He sings, he plays the cello.) Nash claims to have controlled the acoustics of the room with "a new theory of sound". The composer Gioachino Rossini, accompanied by his wife Isabella and a macaw, comes to conduct the King's Band, a forty-six-piece ensemble of wind and percussion, in excerpts from his most popular operas. Astonishingly, he has already, at the age of thirty-one, written thirty-one operas, including *Il Barbiere di Siviglia*. The concert is a success, apart from Gioachino's falsetto rendition of Desdemona's 'Willow Song', from his opera *Otello*, which frightens the audience.

Isabella, seven years older than Gioachino, is an operatic soprano with an astonishing range—three octaves—and a facility for virtuosic singing. She is "a beauty of the most imposing sort", writes Stendhal, "with large features that are superb on the stage, magnificent stature, blazing eyes… and an instinct for tragedy." But a few years later her voice will have deteriorated through overuse and her career will be over. She will take up gambling. Gioachino will cast her aside.

But George and Gioachino are made for each other. Both are ill, ill, always ill; both love sex and food. They sing duets together.

Gioachino writes no IndianMoghulChinese mash-ups. European composers show little interest in Asian music until much later in the nineteenth century. Perhaps this is because architects can, without leaving home, discover and be inspired by Asian culture through books, whereas composers have no access to recordings of Asian music. Nash, who normally designs in a Neo-Classical style and has never travelled to Asia, finds his inspiration for the Pavilion in *Oriental Scenery*, six volumes of aquatints of "hindoo" architecture by the landscape painters Thomas and William Daniell.

The gardens. Plants are imported from Asia and the Americas. The forms of the flowers reflect the Pavilion's domes and towers. Tiger lilies are planted to echo the wallpapers inside.

—

Today, a man is busking in the Pavilion gardens. He plays the mbira, the thumb piano. The instrument, naturally very quiet, has a clever attachment, a shell-shaped piece of metal which amplifies the sound. The music is beautiful, obsessive, slightly irritating. The man is here so often, and for such long periods, that his playing is no longer a performance. It's a facet of everyday life. Two men walk past, tell him to shut the fuck up, go back to his own country. He plays on. His home country is Britain, his home town Brighton.

—

In 1820 George tries to divorce Caroline, claiming that she has committed adultery. Effectively, she is put on trial. A million people sign petitions in her favour. Caroline says to her friends:

"I have indeed committed adultery once, with the husband of Mrs. Fitzherbert." The attempt at divorce fails.

The old king dies and the bullfinches are no longer under instruction. Can they really have learned the tunes of the mechanical organ? Very possibly. "Bullfinches were very gifted mimics of all kinds of tunes", according to the pioneering sound recordist Ludwig Koch. "In France we had one singing the French national anthem *La Marseillaise* very distinctly. There was a bullfinch in Berlin, I never forget it, singing the Communist song *The Red Flag*. And when Hitler came to power in 1933, somebody denounced the owner of the bird. He was arrested, and was released only after the poor bullfinch had been killed. You see, even mimicking birds have to suffer under dictatorship."

George becomes king. He refuses to let Caroline attend the coronation (but he invites his friend from Brighton, the 107-year-old Phoebe Hessel). After the coronation he visits Brighton less often—he is upset by the increasing crowds, for which he, of course, is partly responsible.

George's personal Shampooing Surgeon is Sake Dean Mahomet. Dean has arrived in Brighton in 1814. He has already published a book *The Travels of Dean Mahomet*, about his experience of British colonisation, his travels to Ireland to study English, his interracial, mixed-faith marriage with Jane Daly. (Strangely, he lifts some passages from John Henry Grose's *Voyage to the East Indies*, an unsympathetic account of India.) He has already worked in an Indian bathhouse in London, specialising in *champo*, a head massage with oils, and opened the first Indian restaurant in Britain, the Hindoostanee Coffee House "for the entertainment of Indian gentlemen, where they may enjoy the hoakha, with real Chilm tobacco, and Indian dishes, in the highest perfection, and allowed by the greatest epicures to be unequalled to any curries ever made in England..." What the Hindoostanee Coffee House doesn't serve is coffee.

In Brighton he opens his own bathhouse, with herbal treatments, steam baths, reading rooms, and *champo*: "The Indian Medicated Vapour Bath, a cure to many diseases and giving full relief when everything fails; particularly rheumatic and paralytic, gout, stiff joints, old sprains, lame legs, aches and pains in the joints." The walls are hung with the discarded crutches, spine-stretchers, leg-irons, head-strainers, bump-dressers, and club-foot reformers of cured patients. Dean writes *Shampooing*, a bestselling book. He provides courses of "vegetable pills", "Wooptong baths", "electuaries", "dry cupping", "electrification" (ahead of its time).

He is known as Doctor Brighton—confusingly, since Brighton itself is known as Doctor Brighton. (No need for *champo*, just come down to the coast and you will be cured.)

A vapour bath is installed in the Pavilion. George elevates him to the rank of Shampooing Surgeon.

—

Brighton, City of the Bay (Window).

Brighton doubles itself in a few years, its population and its footprint. Developers, architects, builders—Thomas Read Kemp, Rev. Henry Wagner, Amon Wilds and his son Amon Henry Wilds, Charles Busby, Thomas Cubitt—create an east-west strip. Arriving by boat, it is magnificent, panoramic. "Brighton is all beauty", says William Cobbett.

The development flirts with the sea. It confronts the sea, and then backs off, in the form of crescents and squares, ensuring that more residents can have a view of the precious liquid, the reason for the town's existence. The facades are made of stucco. Colour palette: a thousand shades of cream. The style is freestyle neo-classical, with hints of Gothic, Mughal. Pilasters, pediments, ironwork balconies, verandahs. And crucially, bay windows. The Wave.

It's gloriously pragmatic. Let's get this gorgeous structure up, let's seduce these affluent people—and then we can fill in the details. So first a carcass—basement, foundations, walls, ceiling joists, a roof, openings for windows and doors—like a stage set built to last. And later, the carcass is fleshed out—a well, a drainage system, doors, windows, interior rooms, a back extension for the servants.

Stucco, wood and bungaroosh. The builders sing a Brighton song:

"Roosh roosh roosh roosh
a city built of
bungaroosh
Roosh roosh roosh roosh
let's plug the gaps with
bungaroosh
A wooden frame
will make a wall
just fill the void with
bungaroosh
Broken bricks
some flint and lime
add stones and sand that's
bungaroosh
No one knows
what's under your roof
it's on the cheap it's
bungaroosh"

At one end Brunswick Terrace and Brunswick Square (called after Caroline? a snub to Boy George?). At the other Sussex Square and Lewes Crescent. In between: Bedford Square, Oriental Place, Regency Square, the Royal Albion Hotel, the Royal York Hotel, Marine Square, Eastern Terrace. (Black-tiled Royal Crescent is already there.)

Behind, Amon Henry builds a little sister for the Pavilion, and lives there himself. Thomas commissions Trinity Chapel in Ship Street, Amon designs it, and Thomas preaches there, his own brand of non-conformism. Amon Henry goes into partnership with Henry Phillips, botanist and garden designer. They have plans for an Athenaeum and Oriental Gardens. The design is based on the "celebrated Cave of Elephants" on the Indian island of Salsette. Money runs out. (Later they create The Anthaeum, a spectacular wrought iron and glass conservatory which houses a tropical garden, exotic trees and shrubs, lakes, rockeries. Kew Gardens before Kew Gardens. The day before it is due to open it collapses, spectacularly. The twisted mass of iron sits on the site for twenty years, becomes a tourist attraction.)

And out front, thrusting into the sea, the Suspension Chain Pier. Passengers on the ferry from Dieppe can now disembark without the discomfort of being rowed ashore. What a beautiful idea—a pier which hangs—and it's a tourist attraction too of course, the possibility of walking out over the sea, and of being able to look back at the full glory of the strip, as if arriving by boat.

—

Jo is out on the streets, spray-painting stencilled dogs on the pavement, a trail which leads to our door. A police car roars up, and two policemen get out.

"I'm going to have to book you", says the hard cop, "for defacing the environment".

"Actually I think it's legal", says the (very) soft cop.

"And what about your neighbours? What do they think of this vandalism?"

A neighbour walks past. "We really like these dogs", he says. "They make the neighbourhood a better place."

"Back off. Back off!" says the hard cop. "This a crime scene."

"I don't think it is", says the soft cop.

"Ok, I'm going to let you off with a caution", says the hard cop, "but if I catch you again I won't be so generous".

"You'll have to be", says the soft cop. "What she's doing isn't illegal."

It's the Brighton Festival (and because it's the Brighton Festival it's also time for a giant marquee and the aggressively trashy

*Ladyboys of Bangkok*, kitsch cross-dressing cabaret, which is not a part of the festival but a counterweight to the festival, an act of artistic defiance. Do carry on with your fancy arty stuff, it says to the festival, but what we're doing is closer to the spirit of Brighton, and it's what the real people of Brighton really want to see.) Our house becomes an Open House, *The Dog Show*, for which Jo assembles two hundred works of dog art—paintings, engravings, her own ceramic pieces, sculptures made of wire, of hessian, of wool, of papier mâché, a hound made of plastic milk bottles, a bulldog made of cardboard—and I make cake (oh yes, and dog biscuits, homemade dog biscuits, am I really doing this?) and the house effervesces with people and dogs. Dog drawing upstairs! Dog Photo Booth! Dog Cinema! Most people have come to see the art, some have come to see each other, to eat cake and discuss dogs in minute detail, and some have come to see the house, to inspect it in minute detail, to find out where we bought our windows.

—

Peter and Natasha's house, on the opposite side of our street, is open too. We are gazing at their paintings in the kitchen where we had supper the week before. Their dog Oliver lies catatonic on the floor, recovering from having eaten a small bag of heroin he found under a bush in St Nicholas Rest Garden. The paintings are inspired by John Constable, one of their heroes. Peter and Natasha have just made a discovery: in 1824, Constable lives in this house with his wife Maria and their children. She needs the sea air. She is obliged to live with pulmonary tuberculosis, and bear children at a debilitating rate. Turner, the great J. M. W. Turner, is in town too.

Constable and Turner at Lord Egremont's house in Rock Gardens. (They are both after his patronage.)
"I dislike this town", says Constable.
"The most exciting place in Britain", says Turner.
"Rotten fish", says Constable.
"And fresh ones", says Turner.
"Those hideous amphibious animals the old bathing women", says Constable.

"Indispensable", says Turner.

"Nursery maids, dogs, horses, boys, fishermen", says Constable.

"A marvellous mix", says Turner.

"Ladies dressed—and undressed", says Constable.

"Perfect", says Turner.

"Indecent confusion", says Constable. "There is nothing here for the painter but the breakers—and sky."

And so that is what Constable paints. Here he is on the beach, with sketch book and pencil and paint box. Wooden groynes, mooring posts, capstans, fishing boats, coal brigs; fishermen, women with parasols, customs officers, horses. A mother scoops up her child as he leaps to avoid a wave. Sea and sky, sky and sea. The sky in oranges and browns and pinks and greys and purples. Light on water through shifting masses of rain clouds. Blue and white, green, grey, black seas. "It is the business of a painter not to contend with nature", writes Constable, "but to make something out of nothing, in attempting which he must almost of necessity become poetical."

Turner too paints breakers and sky. But his main task is to paint the town. He has been commissioned by the serialised *Picturesque Views of the Southern Coast of England* to update their images of Brighton, not just in content but in style. He does a brilliant series of views—paintings and sketches—including a cunning watercolour of the front in which he manages to include the Pavilion by choosing a viewpoint way out to sea, beyond the end of the pier.

And Constable and Turner both paint the Suspension Chain Pier. Impossible to resist. It's brand new, it dramatises the seascape, and it's a pet project of Lord Egremont.

—

At 6pm the last dog lover art lover leaves, and we go down to the beach. Light on water through shifting masses of rain clouds. We pull out our mobile phones. No paint box necessary. Horses wander on the beach. Occasionally one breaks into a gallop, jumps over a series of groynes, stops, looks lost.

Boy George dies in 1830 (reconciled to Maria—at his request he is buried with a miniature painting of her eye). "No man clung to life with greater eagerness", says Thomas Raikes, a banker who happens to be a dandy, "or was more unwilling to hear from those about him any hint or suspicion of his apparent decay."

George has given Brighton a reason to exist, beyond mackerel and sea bathing: fun. He's given it a look and a style—exotic, eclectic, flamboyant, hedonistic, badass. "Brighton is still very gay", says Samuel Rogers, a poet who happens to be a banker, "and full of balls."

—

Later, on our way back from Planet India ("authentic home made Indian food made by authentic home made Indians"), we walk past the statue of George outside the Pavilion Gardens. Why make a statue of him? He has a perfectly good monument here already. Two women are spraying a message on to the plinth: END VIOLENCE TO WOMEN. A bullfinch sits on George's head, singing a medley from the *Messiah*.

—

I'm going to make caraway cake from the Martha Gunn Recipe Book. Her writing isn't easy to read. "Take a pound of flower well dryed and a pound of duble refined sugar finely beaten. In sift yr flower and sugar together and take a pound of butter wash it in something and work it in your hands till tis very soft. Mix half yr flower and sugar with yr butter take nine eggs but five of yr whites. Beat them with two somethings of sack" (sack! must get some sack) "then straine yr eggs into yr butter and flower and sugar and stir in the rest of the flower and sugar by degrees and two or three handfuls of carroway seeds" (oof, that's a lot of carroway seeds) "bake it in a something with duble paper under it in oven. Must be quick an hour and quarter will bake. Butter yr something and ice yr cake if you wish."

I walk to the top of our street. Opposite me is Codrington Mansion, where I will buy sugar. The shape of the building is hard to make out because at some moment the front garden has been replaced by a one-storey terrace of shops—now a convenience store, a mobile phone shop, a charity shop, a dry cleaners.

Until recently there was a plaque to Edward Codrington, an admiral who assists Nelson at Trafalgar, becomes head of the Mediterranean fleet and finds himself up to his ears in the Greek War of Independence. He is instructed by the British government to prevent the Ottomans from conquering the Greeks, without taking sides, without firing a shot. At Navarino on the western shore of the Peloponnese in 1827, EC, uninterested in diplomacy, sympathetic to the Greeks, destroys the Ottoman and Egyptian fleets. To the British public, sympathetic to the Greeks, he is a hero. To the British government, terrified by the Russians, he is a pariah—he has compromised the Ottomans' ability to resist the Russians. He is awarded the Grand Cross of Bath—he has to be because of his popularity; but there are subtle repercussions—the refusal to pay his crews the traditional proceeds from the sale of captured Ottoman treasure and goods; and more ruthless repercussions—he is relieved of his command.

In 'The Dream', an 1828 etching by William Heath, EC is the hero. In the background are grateful Greeks and terrified Turks. The Duke of Wellington, recently elected Prime Minister, lies in bed, in the grips of a Medusa-like creature with a black head and dreadlocks, which is torturing him with the anxieties of his new job. Britannia brings EC to his bedside. "He wants no thanks", Britannia says to the Duke. "He has done his duty." EC looks terrified.

He gives his name to several streets in Greece and several pubs in Britain. He comes to live in Brighton, in this mansion owned by his family. What else does his family own? In Antigua they own Betty's Hope, Clare Hall, Room, Garden, Folly, Cotton, Cables, New Work, Bolans, Jennings—

plantations they have converted from tobacco, indigo, ginger to sugar. They also own Barbuda, a small island off Antigua, which supplies the Antiguan plantations with sheep, goats, turtles, and where they make money from salvaging wrecked ships. And they own hundreds of slaves.

Most of these plantations are run by EC's elder brother Christopher Bethell Codrington. EC is joint owner, with two of his other siblings, of Room.

The grocers of Brighton, inspired by Elizabeth Heyrick's pamphlet *Immediate Not Gradual Abolition*, are refusing to stock sugar from the West Indies. George Faithfull, Loyal George, an abolitionist who happens to be a solicitor, a solicitor who happens to be a non-conformist preacher, invites EC to a meeting in the Old Ship Hotel. (In the ballroom Niccolò Paganini is playing something fearsomely fast on the violin. There is a rumour that he has murdered a woman, used her intestines as strings and imprisoned her soul within the instrument. His playing is overlayed with the sound of her screams.) Loyal George makes a passionate speech: Slavery is "repugnant to justice, humanity and sound policy, to the principles of the British constitution and to the spirit of the Christian religion". A petition will be submitted to the Legislature. The Brighton Society for Promoting the Abolition of Slavery and The Ladies Anti-Slavery Association are formed. "So", says George to EC, "what are you going to do?" "Mr. Faithfull", says EC, "I am going to continue the essential work I have been doing, work that has helped to make Britain the great trading nation it is. The result of 'freedom' in my mind would be that in a little time you would have most of them, or perhaps all of them wishing to return to live on the same terms as before."

In 1833 the Slavery Abolition Act is passed. The government compensates EC and CBC for their slaves, and the slaves continue to work for them. Each ex-slave must give forty hours work per week free; any overtime is paid for. EC goes to visit CBC at his mansion Dodington House in Gloucestershire. They settle down to a light supper: fishes, game birds, flummery.

There is a letter from one of CBC's plantation managers, Robert Jarritt: "We have nearly passed the first month of 'freedom' without any violence which is something. At present 'freedom' appears to be the worst thing that could happen to them." In a strange way Jarritt is right—the Abolition Act has declared ex-slaves to be "the inalienable property of their masters".

Now there is no plaque to EC on the front of Codrington Mansion.

I walk back clutching my packet of sugar. Folly!

—

Meanwhile (as I walk home) both Loyal George and EC have become Members of Parliament. EC has abandoned Brighton (too inhospitable?) and has become MP for somewhere or other. The Reform Act has made Brighton into a parliamentary borough, and George has campaigned on a Radical ticket: to end to all "unmerited pensions and sinecures", to reduce the money spent on the Civil List, to disband the army. "All our institutions are partial, oppressive, and aristocratic. We have an aristocratic church, an aristocratic bar, an aristocratic game-code, aristocratic taxation. All is privilege." The Reform Act has given more people the vote (ok, more men—women are explicitly disenfranchised)—butchers and bakers as well as "gentlemen". George and Isaac Newton Wigney, another Radical, are worried that the new voters will be subjected to bribery and intimidation by their employers and landlords. "You who seek to purge and cleanse the system of its present corruption, will you contaminate your fingers with base bribes? Will you be ensnared? No! You cannot, you must not, you will not be guilty of such political debasement. Resist the Devil, and he will flee from you. Spurn the wretch who would thus tamper with your feelings, act as becomes men striving to be free, and success must crown your efforts."

The results:
Isaac Newton Wigney (Radical) 826
George Faithfull (Radical) 720

Captain G. R. Pechell (Whig) 609
William Crawford (Whig) 391
Sir Adolphus J. Dalrymple (Tory) 232

Isaac and George are Brighton's first two MPs. "Some very bad characters have been returned", writes the Whig diarist Charles Greville, "among the worst Faithfull." And George is too radical for the Radicals. He is defeated in the 1835 election. Furious, he founds the newspaper *The Brighton Patriot*—a frisky mixture of Radical politics, society news, and adverts for snake oil.

"To the Radicals we would say, persevere. To the Whigs, reform yourselves. To the Tories, improve."

"Sir Charles Des Voeux is arrived at 72, Brunswick-terrace. Mr. and Mrs. Reed have left 63, Regency-square."

"Presumption and insolence have grown upon the Whigs like those mushroom excrescences which overrun vegetation and stifle life and air."

"The Hon. Mrs. Lamb has taken her departure from the Bedford Hotel; as have Mrs. Lane Fox and Mr. Buckley. The Hon. Twissleton Fiennes will return to Pegg's Royal York Hotel, to-morrow."

"The GENUINE GREASE FROM BEARS shot in Brighton can only be obtained at JAMES LIPSCOMBE, 59, Grand-Parade, which he warrants on oath. This article when obtained genuine will in nine cases out of ten CURE DEAFNESS."

"We perfectly agree that no administration whatever is to be trusted. The people can trust themselves. They know what they need, and what may be conducive to their advantage; but their representatives, and more particularly that portion of them called the government, ought to be suspected by them."

"Her Royal Highness the Princess Augusta will return to Clarence House from Brighton the second week in January."

"GRIMSTONE'S EYE SNUFF. SIGHT RESTORED. NERVOUS HEADACHE CURED."

*The Brighton Patriot* is short-lived.

Loyal George campaigns for the right for women to vote, not in parliamentary elections—the world is not ready—but in local elections. He argues, surprisingly, that only single women with a certain level of income should be given the franchise. He finds himself in surprising company. He has the support of the vicar who happens to be a developer, Rev. Henry Wagner. "I consider it unjust", says Wagner, "that a man should have a vote simply because he is a man, and that a lady should be disenfranchised because she is a lady and the weaker body." But George's former Radical allies, mostly working-class, are outraged. They invite him to a meeting in the Old Ship Hotel. (In the ballroom, Mary Shelley, author of Frankenstein, is reading from her mother Mary's *A Vindication of the Rights of Woman*.) Loyal George is under attack. "The favourite doctrine with Mr. Faithfull seems to be the protection of women" (laughter). "He is as fond of the women as any man in Brighton" (laughter), "but he does not think the polling booth is the proper place for a working woman" (hear, hear). Next day, George makes a five-hour speech to the Privy Council, and the Privy Council rejects his arguments. Women may not vote. "The same objections exist here as elsewhere against females exercising control over public affairs."

And don't imagine that George and Isaac have defined Brighton's politics, even temporarily. In 1837 Sir Adolphus, army officer and arch-Tory, is elected. From 232 votes in 1832 —fickle electorate!

—

In 1850 the monarchy gives up on Brighton. Queen Victoria, who has never liked the Pavilion, empties it of most of its treasures, and sells it to the Corporation of Brighton. The stables become a concert hall. The dome still supports itself. In fact, the building is renamed The Dome. Christabel Pankhurst, Oswald Mosley, Muddy Waters, Winston Churchill, Stevie Wonder, Maya Angelou, David Bowie, *Dark Side of the Moon*. The riding house becomes a Corn Exchange.

Next year Sake Dean Mahomet, whose methods have gone out of fashion, dies forgotten and penniless.

I am painting the ironwork on our verandah. Again. The iron-work is intricate: railings, columns holding up the canopy, ornate brackets—a complex and beautiful construction. It appears robust, but it's engaged in a continuous cold war with rust, and the rust is, continuously, winning. This time I'm optimistic. I've been to a shop called something like Paint Logistic Solutions, and I've bought some exciting black paint which comes from a small room at the back of the shop. No paperwork. Black market black paint! You take the lid off and you swoon as a thousand illegal chemicals envelop you. This gorgeous liquid will revolutionise our lives.

—

City of Rust.

What happens to Brighton while Victoria reigns? Construction, construction, construction. Brighton becomes not a manufacturing town, but a manufactured town, a town which dedicates itself to visitors. It's a theme park. What is the theme? The theme is the sea. The construction is about taming the sea, and making it accessible. Wrought iron, wood and brick on brick on brick. Railings, shelters, bandstands, promenades. (Oh yes, and spectacular sewers. Oh, and a thousand churches. Oh, and most of Hove.)

The train line arrives from London, first class, second class, third class. We cater for everyone. An astonishing viaduct, suspended high above the town, takes the line to Lewes and to Kemp Town. (The solicitor for the train company is Loyal George.)

A radical development: a pier built primarily for pleasure, the West Pier. On the cliff below Kemp Town, a massive covered walkway, Madeira Terrace, with a hundred and fifty arches. A lift to bring you down to the shore. A monumental aquarium, with concert halls and a skating rink.

Magnus Volk, inventor, becomes involved. He has already put

electric lighting into the Pavilion. Now a miniature electric railway takes you from the Aquarium eastwards to the Banjo Groyne (named for its shape, not its sound), and back. Top speed 6mph. Encouraged by its success, Magnus creates the most ambitious attraction of all: out at sea, a pier, no, not a pier, a maritime tram on stilts, "a daddy-long-legs", that moves on tracks on the seabed, four miles from Brighton eastwards to Rottingdean, and back. Top speed 6mph. Very Magnus, but short-lived.

And it's not just about the sea. The countryside must be tamed too. A funicular railway leads up to Devil's Dyke, a dramatic cleft in the Sussex Downs, "perhaps the most grand and affecting natural landscape in the world", according to Constable; and Devil's Dyke becomes Disneyworld: a Steep Grade Railway, an observatory, two bandstands, a camera obscura, fairground rides, an aerial cable railway across the valley. Fun, fun, fun. Short-lived.

Meanwhile the Suspension Chain Pier, built to be useful, but not very useful any more, and—far more reprehensibly—not fun enough, is neglected, allowed to deteriorate, eclipsed by the West Pier. Time for the Marine Palace and Pier—a serious dedicated obsessive palace of fun. The builders are contracted to remove the Chain Pier. But no need—it collapses, finished off by a storm, crashes into the footings of the new pier, a final act of revenge.

—

The Palace Pier is an amusement park, tacky, beautiful. Look at those toll houses at the entrance, rescued from the Chain Pier. Win a teddy bear. Walk on the water—well, walk on those acres of decking, and feel you're walking on water. Hook a duck. Terrify yourself on that turbo coaster. Win another teddy bear. Walk under the pier on the beach, a gorgeous forest of ironwork, and listen to the starlings sing as they roost beneath the decking.

—

Oh, West Pier, what happened?

A place to promenade, to take the sea air, a place of entertainment—a bandstand, landing stages for steamers, a theatre, a concert hall, a restaurant. Now a place for birds.

Neglect, bankruptcy, failed diplomacy, a hurricane (1987, savage), storms, fires. (A fire on a wrought iron structure in the sea? Really? The rumour was, it was the Noble Brothers, who owned the Palace Pier.) Oh, and salt water, the relentless salt water siege.

Many schemes. My brother Piers, the architect with the right name, designed a gloriously ironic one with a skyscraper at the far end—at least I think he did—he doesn't remember. The Noble Brothers opposed these schemes on the grounds of unfair competition.

Do we need two piers?

—

Sheffield 2018. It's my brother Jamie and Nick's civil partnership ceremony. They have sung their vows in Sheffield Town Hall and the two registrars have been in tears and now we are in their garden, and Jamie is making a speech. "I had a miserable teenagehood" (oof, I think, I never noticed); "I thought I would never find love as an adult. There seemed to be no future for people like me. Homosexuality was still illegal. The world seemed to be profoundly against us. And look at us now. Nick and I can live together in a loving relationship, there is no need to hide; in fact we can celebrate it as we are today. This has come about through the struggle of lesbians and gay men. A struggle we must continue!"

—

1844. Edward Carpenter is born in Brunswick Square, of affluent middle class parents who live off the stock market and overseas investments. Aged ten, he starts playing the piano, in secret. Music is not considered suitable for a boy;

there are "six sisters who need to be taught, poor things, whether they like it or not". He composes pieces for the piano but doesn't write them down—he doesn't know how to. He is educated at Brighton College, and at Trinity Hall, Cambridge. He has a flash of revelation: his family's prosperity is built on the misery of the working classes, because there is a socially divisive capitalist system that allows ruling classes to live off the labour of the poor, "consuming much, creating next to nothing". Meanwhile he begins to explore his feelings for men. And these two ideas—socialism and sex—become connected in his mind. He has a vision of total social transformation, "a new world in which men and women of all classes can live creatively together in love, beauty and freedom".

—

When Jamie (born in Brunswick Square) (socialist, activist) (excellent amateur pianist) comes out to me, I am discombobulated. We are both living in Oxford. I bump into him on Magdalen Bridge. Where are you going? I say. To the Cape of Good Hope, he says. Heck, I think, there's a gay disco there! Be careful, I say, you'll get picked up. He grins.

How the hell have I not noticed?

When he comes out to my parents, they are deeply discombobulated. They suspect that sex and socialism are entwined, too entwined, that my brother's left-wing politics have somehow drawn him into being gay. My father, with his experience of teaching in a single-sex boarding school, thinks it's a phase. My mother, who comes from a theatrical background, worries that he will end up a sad middle-aged queen. (They are both entirely wrong.) They say little at the time, but a week later they both write him letters of support.

—

Carpenter becomes a curate, briefly, "as a convention rather than out of deep conviction", and a lecturer in astronomy; but he is frustrated that he is lecturing to the middle class—not a working class student to be seen. He falls in love with Walt

Whitman's poetry. Influenced by Whitman, he has another flash of revelation—"a vibration" through his body: he has to go and make his life with "the mass of the people and manual workers". (Later, he visits Whitman, claims to have had sex with him.) He is sexually attracted to working class men "the grimy and oil-besmeared figure of a stoker", "the thick-thighed hot coarse-fleshed young bricklayer with a strap around his waist".

With the aid of a large inheritance from his father, he buys a plot of land at Millthorpe, in the Cordwell Valley, near Sheffield. It becomes a magnet for socialists, mostly men. They eat porridge and radishes, cultivate a market garden, make sandals, using as a template a pair from India—"a simple life". ("Socialism", writes George Orwell in *The Road to Wigan Pier*, draws to it "every fruit-juice drinker, nudist, sandal-wearer, sex-maniac, Quaker, pacifist and feminist in England.") He has relationships with a giddying series of working-class Georges: Hukin, who marries, to Carpenter's eternal regret; Adams, who is already married; Merrill.

He is interested in a thousand radical ideas—socialism, democracy, vegetarianism, animal rights, women's emancipation, prison reform, naturism, smallholdings, recycling... He starts writing down his music, mostly for the piano. He publishes *Chants of Labour: A Song Book of the People*. He writes an epic poem *Towards Democracy* (a poem called *Towards Democracy*? really? really), influenced by Whitman and by Hindu philosophy, about what he calls spiritual democracy: socialism will bring about a revolution not only in human consciousness but in economic conditions. He writes *Civilisation: Its Cause and Cure*. "Today it is unfortunately perfectly true that Man is the only animal who, instead of adorning and beautifying, makes Nature hideous by his presence." What is needed is "a return to nature and community of human life" and "two movements—towards a complex human communism and towards individual freedom and savagery, balancing and correcting each other".

—

Henry Salt, from an affluent middle class background, has been educated at Eton College and become a teacher there. He meets Carpenter and they become friends. Under Carpenter's influence, he realises that Eton teachers are "but cannibals in cap and gown—almost literally cannibals, as devouring the flesh and blood of animals… and indirectly cannibals, as living by the sweat and toil of the classes that do the hard work in the world". He gets rid of his servants, leaves his job and buys a modest cottage in Surrey. He will write, and he will fight for human rights, for animal rights. He sees this as "an emigration, a romance, a strange new life in some remote antipodes."

Salt's axioms:

"That our present so-called civilisation is only a manner of speaking, and is in fact quite a rude state as compared with what may already be foreseen."
"That the basis of any morality must be the sense of kinship between all living beings."
"That there can be no abiding national welfare until the extremes of wealth and poverty are abolished."
"That warfare will not be discontinued until we have ceased to honour soldiering as heroic."
"That the rights of animals have henceforth to be considered; and that such practices as cruel sports, vivisection and flesh-eating are not compatible with civilised life."

—

In 1889 Mohandas Gandhi comes to Brighton, for a meeting of vegetarians. He meets an old woman in a hotel. He doesn't understand the menu, which is in French. She helps him to choose the vegetarian dishes. He eats boiled potatoes and boiled cabbage. They become friends. She introduces him to a series of young women, including her ward. "She had plans for me." He is confused—he enjoys the meetings, but. Eventually he owns up: he has a wife and son in India. In 1883, aged thirteen, he has married the fourteen-year-old Kasturbai, a marriage arranged by their parents. "We didn't know much about marriage. Our wedding day meant only wearing new clothes, eating sweets and playing with relatives."

Gandhi is a member of the Vegetarian Society, formed in 1847 out of the temperance movement. Recently there has been a schism; the London Vegetarian Society and the Manchester Vegetarian Society are incompatible. London is more hardline than Manchester, where you can be an associate member even if you eat chicken and fish. Gandhi is a London vegetarian. "If anybody said that I should die if I did not take beef tea or mutton, even on medical advice, I would prefer death." He meets Salt. They become friends. The Vegetarian Society has recently published Salt's book *A Plea for Vegetarianism*. Rather than arguing directly for improvements in animal welfare, he makes an ethical plea: "If we are ever going to do justice to the lower races, we must get rid of the antiquated notion of a great gulf fixed between them and mankind, and must recognise the common bond of humanity that unites all living beings in one universal brotherhood."

—

At Planet India tonight (no question of beef tea or mutton here) the authentic home made Indians have cooked up a storm and we're eating Dhai Bhel Puri "a taste sensation, sweet, sour, spicy, soft, crispy, fresh and zesty, all in the same mouthful", and hot mixed pickle, "a crunchy and raunchy pickle full of the weird and wonderful, maybe some lotus root, or maybe something that looks like a pea but isn't?"

—

At Millthorpe, Married George (Adams) is banished, and Carpenter starts a relationship with Young George (Merrill), twenty years his junior. They live together openly. The tolerance would be unlikely were they living further south, where attitudes towards homosexuality are hardening. "Eros is a great leveller. Perhaps the true democracy rests, more firmly than anywhere else, on a sentiment which easily passes the bounds of class and caste, and unites in the closest affection the most estranged ranks of society. It is noticeable how often

Uranians of good position and breeding are drawn to rougher types, as of manual workers, and frequently very permanent alliances grow up in this way, which although not publicly acknowledged have a decided influence on social institutions, customs and political tendencies." (Uranians? gay men. In *A Problem in Modern Ethics*, John Addington Symonds categorises men into four groups: dioning—a heterosexual man; urning—a person who is physically male at birth, has a female psyche, and is mainly sexually attracted to men; uranodioning—a bisexual man; hermaphrodite. A man may move from category to category.)

Salt and his wife Kate have come to live in Millthorpe. Kate is a lesbian, has refused to have sex with him. She admires Carpenter for his championing of homosexuality. Is she in love with him? Salt, a fan of George Adams, is suspicious of Merrill.

E. M. Forster comes to Millthorpe. Merrill "touched my backside—gently and just above the buttocks. I believe he touched most people's. The sensation was unusual and I still remember it, as I remember the position of a long vanished tooth. He made a profound impression on me and touched a creative spring." He is inspired to write a gay novel *Maurice*. Carpenter and Merrill become Maurice Hall and his gamekeeper Alec Scudder. (A gay *Lady Chatterley's Lover*, long before *Lady Chatterley's Lover*.) *Maurice* is eventually published in 1971, ten years after the *Lady Chatterley's Lover* court case, four years after the legalisation of homosexuality.

"Forward rather than back, Edward Carpenter! Edward Carpenter!" writes Forster in his diary. Carpenter goes forward. He writes *Homogenic Love and its Place in a Free Society*, a passionate plea for the acceptance of homosexuality. It is circulated privately. (Later it morphs into *Love's Coming of Age*, and into *The Intermediate Sex*.)

—

Kate dies, and Salt moves to Brighton. Merrill wants town life, so he and Carpenter sell Millthorpe (to a "beast of a millionaire"), and move south, to the outskirts of Guildford. Strange decision. "EC turned up unexpectedly in Brighton a few days ago", writes Salt, "and I had two evenings' talk with him. (GM was with him in lodgings, but did not call here.) He seemed well physically... but in spirits rather depressed, and ready to recant his terrible optimism of the past."

Merrill dies, and Carpenter soon after. Salt writes a eulogy that is not quite a eulogy.

"The gay godfather of the liberal left", Fiona McCarthy calls Carpenter. He is surely the gay godfather of Brighton. Ironic that he left Brighton in disgust.

—

Le Gateau Chocolat (The Man—The Lycra—The Complete Asshole) is singing Wagner, and the audience is loving it.

It's the Brolivier Awards at the Theatre Royal. The Brighton theatre world has gathered to pat itself on the back and eat miniature fish and chips. Everyone is here. Anna Maria Crouch Tim Crouch Rex Harrison Steve Coogan Dora Bryan Alan Melville Neil Bartlett Dion Boucicault Max Miller Cate Blanchett Laurence Olivier Jack Buchanan Terence Rattigan Doris Day Ellen Nye Chart Lesley Manville Daisy and Violet Hilton Jack Tinker Joan Plowright Robin Maugham Tristran Sharps Douglas Byng Elizabeth Robins Paule Constable. The awards are presented by Boy George. "Brighton is a theatre", says Boy George, "and you are its custodians." No one quite knows what this means, but they roar their approval.

Best actor: Laurence Olivier (again!)
Best actress: Anna Maria Crouch (Boy George, with whom she once had a brief affair, hands her a generous cheque)
Best vaudeville act: Daisy and Violet Hilton, conjoined twins (Daisy plays the violin and Violet the saxophone)
Best opera singer who is also a cabaret performer: Le Gateau Chocolat (who is, like many other people in Brighton, gay and, unlike many other people in Brighton, black ("You Brightonians

all think you're so tolerant", says Boy George, "but how come there are so few black people living here?"))
Best newcomer: Elizabeth Robins

At the end Rex Harrison sings (you call that singing?) the Queen song *Brighton Rock*, and the Brighton theatre world disperses, euphoric.

—

Elizabeth Robins is born in Kentucky in 1862. Against her parents' wishes, she becomes an actor, and joins the Boston Museum Company. Her husband George Parks, an actor too, jealous of her success, infuriated by her refusal to give up, jumps into the Charles River in a suit of theatrical armour, drowns himself.

She comes to London, specialises in Ibsen. She plays the lead role in the first London performance of *Hedda Gabler*: "one of the most notable events in the history of the modern stage", says the *Sunday Times*. Influenced by Ibsen's *Ghosts*, she and Florence Bell create *Alan's Wife*, a radical reworking of Medea, adapted from a short story by Elin Ameen, about Jean, a working-class woman who murders her child. Jean's husband Alan's mangled body is brought home to her after an industrial accident. She gives birth to a disabled child. She loves him, is repulsed by him, murders him as an act of mercy. "I've had courage just once in my life", she says, "just once in my life have I been strong and kind—and it was the night I killed my child!" Elizabeth plays Jean. "A Rescue Society should be formed without delay for the purpose of reclaiming Miss Elizabeth Robins from the slimy clutches of those who find pleasure in pictures of the charnel house, the dissecting room, or the hospital ward", writes WM, whoever he may be. "Has a woman the right to lay bare the inmost fibres of her being before a gaping playhouse crowd?" writes A. B. Walkley, a civil servant who happens to be the theatre critic of the *Times*.

Elizabeth becomes a suffragette, arrives in Brighton, meets Octavia Wilberforce, great granddaughter of William Wilberforce, abolitionist.

—

Aged ten, I am obsessed with cricket. If I could play cricket every moment of every day, I would. I will play in the rain, I will play in the snow. The only books I read are books about cricket. I go often to see the Sussex County Cricket Club play at their ramshackle ground in Hove. (Sometimes I bump into Dusty. She has come to visit her parents who live round the corner. "Cricket", she says, "I just love the fact that you love cricket. The most boring game in the world!") A small park, no, a massive lawn surrounded by a shanty town of low-rise spectator terraces, huts, offices, cafés, spaces for indoor practice. A pavilion, not a Boy George pavilion, a practical pavilion, for the players. The ground is overlooked by rows of red-brick Victorian houses and a couple of high-rise housing blocks (get those binoculars out!). We are inside the city, and outside it, in a hermetic world. Most people coming in here would have no idea what is going on; we are members of a benevolent cult. I'm here, watching avidly, filling in my score book, surrounded by old men. I am enthralled by John Snow, a fast bowler who happens to be a poet. I am fascinated by the Nawab of Pataudi, who bats exquisitely despite a right eye damaged in a car accident. He is the first Indian person I have ever seen, though he is by no means the first Indian person to play for Sussex.

Ranji.

There is a film of him batting in the nets in Hove. It's 1897. He dances, he darts, he skips, he skitters. He crashes the ball into the side netting, flicks it behind him with his signature shot, the leg glance. There is no question of defence. It feels like a performance. Is he playing to the camera? In matches he uses defensive shots, but not many. He is an attacking batsman. He scores thousands of runs, and he scores them quickly.

Back a few years. The Maharajah of Nawanagar has fourteen wives but no sons. He decides to adopt a boy, the grandson of one of the officers in his army. It's not entirely clear whether this adoption ever takes place, but Ranji certainly becomes the Maharajah's ward. His status rises, and he receives a privileged education which finishes with a spell at Trinity College, Cambridge. He doesn't complete his degree; he concentrates on tennis, cricket, billiards. He plays cricket for the university, despite opposition to the idea of an Indian in the team. As an upper-caste Indian, he is, nearly but not quite, an honorary Englishman.

He meets Mohandas Gandhi. Gandhi is an underarm lob bowler with a vicious break from leg. They watch cricket together. Ranji tires of Gandhi's pretentious commentary on the game. No, actually, this doesn't happen. It is an invention of the writer Ian Buruma in his novel *Playing The Game*. In fact Gandhi has no interest in cricket.

Ranji meets C. B. Fry, athlete, footballer, boxer, golfer, tennis player, cricketer, a man who has his own magazine in which he writes about men's fashions, Esperanto, safety razors, map reading, phrenology, and promotes women's cricket. Ranji and CB become friends. CB is playing for Sussex, so Ranji decides to play for Sussex too. He comes to Hove. He is hugely popular—no wonder, he transforms the fortunes of a mediocre team. Part of his attraction is his exoticism, his flamboyant, wristy technique of batting. He combines an Oriental calm with an Oriental swiftness, writes the journalist A. G. Gardiner, the stillness of a panther with the suddenness of its spring. When Ranji bats, writes Neville Cardus (a man who like me has two obsessions, music and cricket), a strange light from the East flickers in the English sunshine.

(Years later the choreographer Shobana Jeyasingh comes to Brighton to study at Sussex University. She completes her degree in English, and starts performing traditional Bharatanatyam dance. Her audiences love her for her exoticism. She brings India to them in an agreeable form that doesn't threaten. Shobana, a very different person from Ranji, becomes increasingly dissatisfied with this adulation, and begins to make more and more radical work in which Bharatanatyam goes head to head with Western modern dance. It's tempting to call it a glorious hybrid, but it's more interesting than that, as there is always, intentionally, a tension between the forms.)

Ranji and CB are the beating heart of the Sussex team. They play in contrasting styles—CB is orthodox, technically precise—but they are equally prolific run-scorers.

Ranji plays in a Gentlemen v. Players match at Lords. The Gentlemen are upper-class players who are amateurs, unpaid even when they play for England; the Players are working-class professionals, paid to play, even when they're playing for local club teams. Ranji plays for the Gentlemen. In the first innings he makes 47 in 12 balls against a fearsome bowling line-up, and 51 not out in the second. "One of the most brilliant and delightful pieces of batting seen at Lords", says Wisden, the bible of cricket. (John Wisden, Brightonian, has himself had a successful career playing for Sussex as an extremely fast round-arm bowler, and a successful business selling cricket equipment and cigars.)

Now, the moment has arrived. Ranji is considered for the national team. Surely not? An Indian playing for England? Yes, an Indian soldier can be co-opted into the British army, but this is different isn't it? If England cannot win without resorting to the assistance of coloured individuals of Asiatic extraction, say the old men, it had better devote its skills to marbles. He has never played a Christian stroke in his life, say the old men.

Lord Harris agrees. Six years ago he was Governor of Bombay. Now he is responsible for choosing the team for the Lords Test match against Australia. He refuses to pick Ranji, a "bird of passage". The press and the public debate this decision enthusiastically. For the Manchester Test match, Lord Harris has no say. Ranji, under consideration, insists that the Australians be consulted before the final selection. The Australian captain is delighted, so Ranji plays. He makes an uncharacteristically cautious 62 in tricky circumstances in the first innings, and an exquisite 154 not out in the second. Ranji has arrived. No question of leaving him out of the team now.

He becomes captain of the Sussex team, experiments with tactics which upset his teammates, takes up bowling, becomes (slightly) more careful in his batting style, makes runs brilliant runs more runs for Sussex and England.

—

Thursday afternoon. Milo comes home.
"How was school?" we say.
"Good", he says.
"How did the cricket go?"
"Ya, good."
"Did you win?"
"Ya."
"Did you take any wickets?"
"Er, ya."
"How many?"
"Six."
"Wow, well done."
"Well, five of them were in my first over. Actually, it was the first over of the match."
"Whaaaaat?" I'm thinking, that's possibly a world record. Wisden must be informed! And we missed it.
"But you told us not to come and watch! You said it would be boring."
"Yes, well, don't always do what I tell you."
We had better remember to go and watch when he plays for England, I think. He doesn't.

—

As his cricketing career ebbs, Ranji, with a protracted campaign of diplomacy and the support of the British government, becomes Maharajah Jam Saheb of Nawanagar. In a glorious homage | act of cultural appropriation, he transforms the capital city Jamnagar into Brighton. Indian architecture inspired by an Englishman's sketchy idea of the architecture of India—a hall of mirrors. Ranji is more interested in entertaining than in ruling. The local people feel he is idle, uncaring, addicted to luxury, too pro-British.

He becomes the Indian representative in the League of Nations. He takes on CB as his deputy, and delegates most of the work to him. They travel across Europe, through the Balkans to Turkey. CB wants to see the war between the Turks and the Greeks at first hand, so they risk their lives hunting for battlefields. CB turns down an offer to become King of Albania. The Albanians, he writes in his autobiography, sent a delegation and appointed a Bishop, who bore a striking resemblance to (the legendary cricketer) W. G. Grace—award-winning beard, presumably—to find an English country gentleman with £10,000 a year for their King. I had the first qualification but not the second. But if I had really pressed Ranji to promote me, it is quite on the cards that I should have been King of Albania yesterday, if not today.

(No one has ever been quite sure whether to believe this story, particularly as it was endorsed by Neville Cardus, who, like me, is sometimes accused of inventing facts.)

At the 1922 General Election CB stands as the Liberal candidate for Brighton. His campaign is boosted by the appearance of his friend Clara Butt (Dame Clara Butt!) at a hustings meeting. She sings Dusty's *I Can't Make It Alone*. Does she? Does she? But the Conservative and Unionist Party has a powerful candidate—in fact they have two powerful candidates, running against each other (or are they running with each other?), the Right Honourable George Clement Tryon and Sir Alfred Cooper Rawson. GCT 28,549; ACR 26,355; CB 22,059; brave but doomed.

CB's mental health deteriorates. Ranji and CB visit India. CB begins to have paranoid episodes. He believes that an Indian has cast a spell on him. He takes against Ranji. Their friendship is at an end.

CB becomes a fan of Hitler and Mussolini. He visits Germany in 1934 aiming to forge links between the Boy Scouts and Hitler Youth. He meets Joachim von Ribbentrop the Nazi Foreign Minister and tries to persuade him that the Third Reich should take up cricket. Training players to Test match standard "would have a wonderful effect on the direction of the Führer's desires."

—

2010
Election day. Off go Jo and I to the New Venture Theatre to make our marks. People from all parts of society are making their way there too, to vote alongside us, in agreement with us, in disagreement, in hope, in disgust, in disillusion. This fleeting opportunity to affect the future. Vote vote vote for Caroline Lucas. A woman, a radical socialist, who doesn't bombard us with lies, who doesn't try to set one half of the nation against the other, who realises that we live in an anthropocene age.

—

1907
In the Dome, Christabel Pankhurst addresses a large gathering of women's societies and groups. Clementina Black is there, Millicent Fawcett, Minnie Turner, Eva Bourne, Mary Leigh, Emma Newsam. "Deeds, not words", says Christabel Pankhurst. The suffrage movement has made some progress, but radical action is needed.
"Rise up women for the fight is hard and long", the women sing. Not everyone is convinced. Millicent Fawcett, who has for forty years been passionately campaigning with words (she made a speech at a pro-suffrage meeting in Brighton in 1870), is worried about the implications of the word "deeds". She resolves to support the movement "only by argument, based on common sense and experience and not by personal violence or lawbreaking of any kind".

The Brighton branch of the Women's Social and Political Union, the WSPU, is formed. Its offices are above the Singer Sewing Machine Company.

Elizabeth Robins writes a play *Votes for Women*, in which Vida Levering is liberated by the realisation that her personal problems are at least partly a result of the economic and political subjugation of women. The whole of the second act is set at a women's suffrage rally in Trafalgar Square. "Half-hour or so of the most brilliantly forcible, lively, shrewd, and humorous platform oratory on the suffrage question", writes the (anonymous) *Daily Chronicle* reviewer, "yards of glorious irrelevance." Elizabeth rejects sexual advances from her publisher William Heinemann and from George Bernard Shaw—"his avowed feminism is specious". She warns them off with a gun.

Twenty suffragettes are ejected from a meeting in the Dome chaired by the Education Minister Reginald McKenna, using, says the *Brighton Herald*, "gentle ju-jitsu". One has "a voice with a shrill squeak as though she were fleeing frightened from a nightmare of mice." Another "must have been crossed in love, or she would never have wasted her charms on the desert air of a suffragette riot". (A message from the *Brighton Herald* to the suffragettes: your work is essential.)

1909
Emmeline Pankhurst's younger sister Mary Clarke becomes the head of the Brighton branch of the WSPU.

1910
Eva Bourne and Mary Leigh are at the Dome. "We are here to decorate the platform for Mrs. Pankhurst's meeting", they tell the custodian. They hide in the organ, intending to disrupt a speech by the Prime Minister Herbert Asquith, nominally a Liberal, who is relentlessly hostile to women's suffrage. The custodian hears a sneeze. He climbs awkwardly into the organ. The two women are arrested. "We are thinking of bringing a counter-charge about the horribly dusty condition of the organ", they say to one of the policemen.

The next day, Emma Newsam dresses up in her husband's clothes, her hair tucked up under a flat cap, and goes to the meeting. When Asquith mentions the word "justice", she stands up, revealing her long hair and long skirt, demanding justice for women.

Minnie Turner's boarding house Sea View, overlooking the sea, is a refuge for suffragettes recovering from imprisonment, hunger strikes and forced feeding.

On November 18th, Black Friday, suffragettes marching to Parliament are attacked by police for six hours, beaten, punched, groped, thrown to the ground. The *Daily Mirror* publishes a photograph of Ada Wright lying collapsed on the ground, hands clutching her face. The government tries, unsuccessfully, to have the paper removed from sale. The Home Secretary Winston Churchill refuses to allow a Government enquiry.

The suffragettes decide on their response: window-smashing. "The argument of the broken window pane is the most valuable argument in modern politics", says Emmeline Pankhurst.

A few days later Mary Clarke is arrested for smashing a window. "Prison is the only place for self-respecting women", she says.

Mary Clarke is released from prison, where she has been on hunger strike, and has been force-fed. She dies two days later, on Christmas Day. "She is the first to die", writes Emmeline Pankhurst. "How many must follow", she says to Asquith, "before the men of your party realise their responsibility?"

1911
Minnie Turner is arrested for breaking a window in the Home Office. She is imprisoned for twenty-one days in Holloway Prison.

1912
Clementina Black, co-founder of the Women's Trade Union Association, author of *Sweated Industry and the Minimum Wage*, becomes editor of suffragette paper *The Common Cause*, so

called because "humanity is bi-sexual, in other words there are not 'women's causes' and 'men's causes'".

Minnie Turner joins the Tax Resistance League. (Members of the league refuse to pay taxes until they are allowed to vote.) Her goods are seized and sold at auction in lieu of tax.

Elizabeth Robins leaves the WSPU. She finds the Pankhursts' leadership too dictatorial, their activism too violent.

1913
Minnie Turner receives a postcard from What Ho Alf, threatening to break her windows, which he does. "Masculine logic", she says. "Imitation is the sincerest form of flattery."

The Cat and Mouse Act. Persecution. Hunger-striking suffragettes are released from prison for enough time to recover their health before returning to serve their sentence. Elizabeth Robins invites the persecuted women to her farmhouse outside Brighton to recuperate and hide from the police.

—

In 1914 the Pavilion is converted, in two weeks, into a military hospital for Indian soldiers. It is thought they will feel at home here. (But it's a palace!) There are 600 beds, there is X-ray equipment, there are two operating theatres, one of them in the kitchen. There is a lot of lino. There are Hindu taps and Muslim taps. Nine kitchens are set up in the gardens so food can be cooked in many styles. For Sikhs there is a Gurdwara in a tent. Muslims can pray on the eastern lawns.

For the military authorities, it is a propaganda dream. Official photographers are invited to the Pavilion to photograph immaculately dressed patients sitting up happily in spotless beds under glamorous gilded ceilings.

The king and queen visit the hospital to present the Victoria Cross to Mir Dast, who has heroically rescued wounded Indian and British officers under heavy fire at Ypres. "The gas has done for me", says Dast later. "I had rather not have been gassed than get the Victoria Cross." His brother, Mir Mast, has meanwhile, no one knows why, led a small band of men to defect to the Germans.

The Pavilion patients are invited to people's houses, taken sightseeing. They go out on the town, are spotted in lowlife dives. From now on they are chaperoned. The Pavilion gardens are fenced in with barbed wire. The women of Brighton must be protected from "khaki fever".

—

Shobana and I have an idea: we will make a piece in the kitchen of the Pavilion. Choreography of colonialisation and cookery. Dancers leaping over wooden tables! Kedgeree, bhel puri! Spicy, fresh, zesty! Perhaps there will be a cameo for Martha Gunn. No, says the Pavilion, which is now a museum. Health and safety. The idea goes on my tottering pile of Unrealised Ideas.

—

In 1918 The Representation of the People Act enfranchises women, partially, partially. Only women of a certain age, with a certain level of income, are given the franchise. At Sea View there is cautious jubilation.

And women may become members of parliament. Britain elects its first female MP later that year, the radical socialist Constance Markievicz, of Sinn Féin, who has recently emerged from a prison sentence for her part in the Easter Rising and is back in Holloway Prison for opposing conscription. (In accordance with Sinn Féin policy, she doesn't take her seat in the House of Commons.) Brighton elects its first female MP ninety-two years later: Caroline Lucas.

—

After the war Elisabeth Robins campaigns for the right of single women to adopt children. She works for the Association for Social and Moral Hygiene, "to promote a high and equal standard of morality and sexual responsibility for men and women", and for the Six Point Group, to promote six points of gender equality: political, occupational, moral, social, economic, legal. She converts her farmhouse into a rest home for "overfatigued professional and activist women and mothers", and moves in with Octavia Wilberforce.

Octavia wants to "mean something in the world"; against her parents' wishes she has decided to become a doctor. Her father has refused to pay for her to study medicine. Elizabeth has stepped in and paid the fees, and Octavia has become a doctor. "Meeting Elizabeth", says Octavia, "was a turning point in my life—hero worship at first sight." They live together for forty years, at 24 Montpelier Crescent, from which Octavia runs her practice. They adopt a daughter, Margaret. Are they lesbians? Who knows? They are women who don't feel the need to hitch themselves to a man.

They meet Leonard and Virginia Woolf. Virginia's novel *Orlando*, in which Orlando lives for several hundred years and transforms from man to woman, a novel about the possibility of being many selves, has just been published. Elizabeth describes Virginia as "probably the greatest living writer of English prose". Years before, Virginia has reviewed, anonymously, Elizabeth's novel *A Dark Lantern*, about a woman recovering from mental illness and the manipulative doctor who supervises her; Virginia has found Elizabeth's writing conventional and "brutal"—though their views of the world are very similar.

Octavia tries to help Virginia to deal with her recurrent mental illness. On March 27th 1941 Leonard drives Virginia to consult Octavia in Brighton. Octavia examines her (curiously, it's a physical examination), and advises complete rest. The next day, Virginia walks into the River Ouse with stones in her pockets.

—

I have a BUPA check-up, and I am anxious about my body (though not tempted to transform from man to woman). Off

I go to 24 Montpelier Crescent, Seven Dials Medical Centre.
All the doctors are men.
"My left thigh", I say. "My prostate. My heart. My voice."
"Oh God", says Dr. Sadler, "you've had a BUPA check-up,
haven't you?" and patiently, tetchily (can one be patient and
tetchy at the same time?) starts to address my anxieties.

—

Vesta Tilley, matchless, named after a match and a virgin
goddess, is dressed as a man. She is standing on the balcony
of her flat in St. Aubyn's Mansions, overlooking the sea, eating
cockles and drinking Assam Tea.

Clara Butt is dressed as Britannia. She is 6ft 2in. She is on the
balcony of her flat in St. Aubyn's Mansions, overlooking the
same sea, eating oysters and drinking Earl Grey Tea.

When she has finished her cockles Vesta, in the person of
Pocket Sims Reeves, sings *The Anchor's Weighed*. She is a
soprano; her voice is clear and agreeable, though thin. But
that's not the point. The point is her pitch-perfect impersona-
tion of Pocket Sims Reeves.

When she has finished her oysters Clara sings *Where Corals
Lie* from Edward Elgar's song cycle *Sea Pictures*. She has two
voices. Her chest voice is deep, resonant, booming—so deep
that you could mistake it for a man's. On a clear day, you
can hear her across the channel, says the conductor Thomas
Beecham. Her head voice is much softer, delicate. She nose-
dives from head voice to chest voice like an exhibition pilot at
an air show. Her voice is obscene, says the composer Reynaldo
Hahn.

Vesta, in the person of Burlington Bertie, sings *Burlington
Bertie*. Her hair is tightly plaited.

Clara's husband Bertie comes out on the balcony and sings
something-or-other in his passable baritone; but we're not
interested in him.

Clara is a devout Christian Scientist. She will contract spinal cancer and spend the later part of her life in a wheelchair. Her faith will give her strength.

Vesta is many men. She is a policeman, a judge, a soldier, a clergyman. She sings *The Piccadilly Johnny with the Little Glass Eye*. She has successfully taken a transgressive act and made it into a mainstream success. Women love her for her independence, for the seductive idea of freedom she has put into their heads; working class men love her for satirising the upper classes.

Clara is a member of the upper classes. She has given her name to a tulip. She sings *The Lost Chord* by Arthur Sullivan.

Vesta, wearing khaki fatigues, sings *The Army of Today's Alright*. During the World War 1, performing at the variety theatres such as the London Coliseum, she has successfully seduced hundreds of men into enlisting, including an entire battalion known as The Vesta Tilley Platoon.

Clara sings *There Is No Death*. Both her sons will die before her, one of meningitis, the other by shooting himself.

Vesta's husband Walter decides to run for Parliament. Vesta abandons her career to devote herself to promoting his—and to avoid embarrassing him. Her farewell tour lasts a year. Walter becomes, nominally, MP for Blackpool, but he only attends parliament twice a year, once on Budget Day and once during Royal Ascot.

Vesta sings *I'm Glad I've Got a Bit of a Blighty One*, a song about the relief of being invalided home.

Clara sings *Abide With Me*. The chest voice, the head voice. The heart, the head, the chest. Where is the voice?

A crowd gathers below the balcony. Boy George, Dusty, Poison Girls, Nick Cave, Jack Buchanan, MarthaGunn (the entire band), David Gilmour, Isabella Rossini, Le Gateau Chocolat,

Bat for Lashes… It's a masterclass. Led by Clara, they sing *Land of Hope and Glory*. Led by Vesta, they sing *Jolly Good Luck To The Girl Who Loves A Soldier*. Their enthusiasm for the two great women's performing skills, their sense of having been educated in the art of singing overwhelms them. They throw bouquet after bouquet up onto the balconies.

Hope and glory.

—

Afterwards Vesta is in conversation with Phoebe Hessel, who has spent seventeen years of her life dressed as man. They are discussing the evolution of army uniform.

In 1728, at the age of fifteen, Phoebe Hessel joins the army to fight alongside her lover Samuel Golding | because her mother has died and her father, called up, can't look after her, so teaches her the fife and drum and takes her with him. She stays in the army until she is wounded at the Battle of Fontenoy, a British triumph | a British disaster. She reveals her sex to the colonel's wife | her sex is revealed when she is obliged to remove her tunic to receive a whipping. She marries Samuel, has nine children of whom eight die in infancy, and comes to live in Brighton when Samuel dies. She sells fish, she sells oranges, she sells gingerbread, she grows old. "Other people die", she says. "I cannot." At the age of 107 she attends Boy George's coronation parade.

"How did you keep your secret?" says Vesta.
"I told my secret to the ground", says Phoebe. "I dug a hole, and whispered it there. How did you keep yours?"
"Oh, it was no secret", says Vesta. "People had to know I was a woman. They revelled in the fact that I was a woman pretending to be a man. But I wanted to be as authentic as I could. I wore men's underwear. That was a huge help. It meant I carried myself like a man."
Clara comes to join them.
"Clara", says Vesta, "this is Phoebe, who has been a man and a woman. She loved your performance."

"You were brilliant", says Phoebe. "You sounded like a man and a woman, in the same body."

"Oh for fuck's sake", says Clara, and goes off to get a drink.

—

We go walking in the Accursed Mountains in northern Albania, unimaginably beautiful, wild, macho, poverty-stricken. A culture of hospitality and blood feuds. (And burrnesha: women who take a vow of chastity in order to live as men; they dress as men, they work in men's jobs, they *become* men.) This is the area from which men, macho men born as men, are coming to Brighton to deal cocaine. Unimaginable wealth, bling, blood feuds, money laundering.

—

When does Brighton start to become bad? When does it move from being a place where there may be some bad people (such as Henry Fauntleroy, a banker who lives in splendour at the top of our street, until he is hung, the last person in Britain to be hung for fraud) to being a place where bad stuff *will* happen, "a town", says the writer Keith Waterhouse, "that looks as if it is constantly helping the police with their enquiries"?

Let's find out by reading some fiction.

The writer Patrick Hamilton grows up in Hove, at first in a large semi-detached house, then, because his father is not only an alcoholic but a financial incompetent, in a series of boarding houses. Meanwhile his father sleeps off hangovers in his London chambers, spends time with his mistress, becomes an admirer of Mussolini. Patrick, disillusioned by capitalism, becomes a Marxist. Capitalism, he realises, has led directly to the growth of violence and fascism in Europe. He too becomes an alcoholic— "he needs whisky like a car needs petrol"—but he writes several brilliant dark misanthropic novels, *Hangover Square*, *The Slaves of Solitude*, *Twenty Thousand Streets Under the Sky*, a savage satire on capitalism *Impromptu in Moribundia*, and two very success- ful crime thrillers—*Rope*, *Gas Light*—plays which are made into films. Eventually he becomes disillusioned with Marxism.

His last three novels are a trilogy, featuring Ernest Ralph Gorse, child-man, man-child—Brighton fictional scumbag no.1—inspired (is that the right word?) by the real-life con-man and murderer Neville Heath, executed a few years before. Gorse is a trickster, a man who revels in deception. His victims are women. He insinuates himself into their lives with his easy confidence, his apparent generosity, his stories.

The first novel in the trilogy is *The West Pier*, set in 1921. Three middle class eighteen-year-olds, Ryan, unusually good-looking, Bell, spectacled, pipe-smoking, and Gorse, the leader, have been at school together in Brighton. There they meet two working-class girls ("birds") Esther Downes, spectacularly pretty, and her sidekick Gertrude Perks, spectacled, plain. Gertrude has "the self-conscious stiffness of a chained, alert macaw being too closely stared at on a perch at the zoo". She tries to manoeuvre Bell into a relationship—and fails. (She eventually marries a fishmonger.) Esther, who works in a sweet shop, comes from a ferociously poor background. She lives near the train station, in Over Street—shabby, down-at-heel, embarrassing. (Now a crucial cog in the charm of the North Laine.)

Ryan falls in love with Esther, or rather with Esther's looks, and Gorse sets to work: a patient, ruthless campaign to poison Ryan and Esther's relationship. He sends Esther an anonymous threatening letter, and when she, horrified, shows it to him, he says "This obviously comes from a very low quarter, and the type of person that doesn't stop at anything—anything—do you understand? I don't think you know the shadier side of life. How should you? I happen to have come across them—on racecourses, and other places. And the bad part of Brighton's as bad as any place on earth."

The Brighton of *The West Pier* is a place of tacky hotels, run-down boarding-houses, amusement arcades and candy floss. The Pier itself, the centre of the action, is a "sex-battle-ship". Esther likes "walking on the Pier for its own sake... its lights, its band, its slot machines, its smell of tar, its rusty foundations, its noise of people's footsteps clacking incessantly on wood just above the satin-surfaced sea, its curious iron-grille quadrangle at the end, and its vast views of twinkling Brighton and Hove... and it's free for anyone to go on, ain't it?" But the Pier is "intimately and intricately connected with the entire ritual of 'getting off'...". An invitation to go on the Pier is "like an invitation to dance". It almost confers upon "getting off" an air of respectability.

Gorse insinuates himself into Esther's affection by buying her cocktails at the Hotel Metropole. Esther reveals she has a stash of money hidden in her bedroom, and Gorse falls in love, falls in love with Esther's stash. Now he has two missions: to see off Ryan, and to relieve Esther of her money. Obsessively, viciously, cunningly, he succeeds in both.

—

Brighton, City of Sex.

How to get a divorce. It has to be about adultery.

So

the husband hires a private detective. He goes down to Brighton (it has to be Brighton), hires a sex-worker and a hotel room. The private detective notes down their comings and goings. Afterwards inspects the sheets.

The wife takes the husband to court.

(When Neil Jordan makes a film of the Graham Greene's *The End of the Affair* he puts in a Brighton scene, not in the novel, in which a divorce is engineered in precisely this way.)

—

Grahame Greene describes *The West Pier* as "the best book written about Brighton". He is in a perfect position to be magnanimous, as he has written the book that most people think is the best book written about Brighton: *Brighton Rock*.

In Greene's earlier novel *A Gun for Sale* Kite, the leader of a gang which extorts money from bookmakers in return for protection, has his throat slit by the rival Colleoni gang. In *Brighton Rock*, set in the mid-1930s, Pinkie Brown, "the Boy", child-man, man-child, Brighton fictional scumbag no.2, is now leader of the gang: Dallow, Cubitt, Spicer. He is charmless, prim, seething with resentment against "them"—the Colleoni gang, the police, the world.

Hale, a journalist who has been used by Colleoni to expose a slot machine scam by the Kite gang, arrives in Brighton. He distributes cards for a newspaper game, a competition to find cards hidden round the town, and to find and identify Hale himself, playing a person called Kolley Kibber. "Hale knew, before he had been in Brighton three hours, that they meant to murder him." He meets Ida Arnold, entertainer, middle-aged, optimistic, compassionate (her compassion is "merciless"). Why is this man so terrified? she thinks.

Pinkie murders Hale ("the word murder conveyed no more to him than the word box, collar, giraffe"), is immediately paranoid, tries to cover his tracks. He sends Spicer out to distribute the Kolley Kibber cards. Rose, a waitress, gentle, gullible, naïve, (Rose, meet Esther, Esther, meet Rose) sees Spicer leaving a card under a tablecloth. Pinkie pursues Rose. He finds her repulsive, but needs must. She is ready to be deceived. "She took deception with such hopeless ease that he could feel a sort of tenderness for her stupidity…" They get married. Rose accepts that she has married a murderer. She persuades Pinkie to make a record of his voice at a fairground booth. "God damn you, you little bitch", he says into the machine, "why can't you go back home for ever and let me be?" Rose cherishes the record, but has no gramophone to play it on.

Ida, suspicious, pursues Pinkie, tries unsuccessfully to persuade Rose that Pinkie is dangerous. Pinkie murders Spicer. "I suppose I'm real Brighton", he says, as if his single heart contained all the cheap amusements, the Pullman cars, the unloving weekends in gaudy hotels, and the sadness after coition."

The final scene, on the cliffs at Peacehaven, is baroque. Afterwards, Rose goes home determined to listen to the record.

The Brighton of *Brighton Rock* is a place of tacky hotels, run-down boarding-houses, amusement arcades and candy floss. A town with an alluring surface: "The holiday crowd… came by train from Victoria every five minutes, rocked down Queen's Road standing on the tops of the little local trams, stepped off in bewildered multitudes into the fresh and glittering air: the new silver paint sparkled on the piers, the cream houses ran away into the west like a pale Victorian watercolour; a race in miniature motors, a band playing, flower gardens in bloom below the front, an aeroplane advertising something for the health in pale vanishing clouds across the sky." But a town with a threatening, sleazy heart: "the mean street, the dustbins along the pavement, the vast shadow of the viaduct", a town in the grip of scumbags.

—

Thundering hooves. A stampede of horses races through Kemp Town. Esther Downes is in the lead. Boy George is near the back of the pack. The pavements are packed with people, and we are shouting and shouting. We've all got money riding on this.

—

Greene bases the Colleoni gang on the Sabini gang from Clerkenwell. The leader, Charles Sabini, uses many first names, including those of his brothers. He is Octavius Sabini, he is Frederick Handley, he is Darby Sabini, he is Thomas Handley. The gang runs a simple protection scam—every bookie must pay the Sabinis for a pitch, and buy equipment from them, equipment they don't need—makes loans to people with bad debts, supplies bodyguards, clerks, ticktack men for illegal bookies. It has the support of police, of judges, of politicians. When World War Two breaks out, Sabini is arrested at Hove Greyhound Stadium, and interned as an enemy alien, despite his mixed Italian and English parentage, and his inability to speak Italian. After the war, his empire is taken over by the White gang. He becomes a smalltime bookie in Brighton.

*Brighton Rock* is made into a film. The film set has an advisory gangster Carl Ramon, ex-Sabini. "He had very thick plastered-down black hair", says Richard Attenborough, who plays Pinkie, "and he taught me how to slash a razor... you can't think of anything more horrific."

—

Hang on, hang on, sorry sorry, what *is* Brighton Rock? Have you ever had Brighton Rock? Pathé News. Information please. Di dum di dum, di doo di dah di doh (jaunty music with a fairground feel). This is the story of two words: BRIGHTON, ROCK—how they find their way into the heart of a favourite confection? Di dum di da di dum di da di dum di doo... Here's the lettering department. Thin strips of red and white sweet stuff are cut to length and fitted together one by one so the visible ends form the outline of a letter. Di da da, di dum dididi da. All the individual letters are assembled into a single slab. The separate lumps of sweet spelling BRIGHTON and ROCK are wrapped around a centre of white sweet. Di da di da di doo. It's rolled into shape, like a huge swiss roll. All hands to the pulley, the lump is raised at one end to be stretched—a hundred and sixty yards of succulent sweet that started as a lump not much longer than a walking stick. Chop, chop, nine hundred and sixty six-inch lengths of rock, and all the way through a message spelling paradise to every child: BRIGHTON ROCK. Dummmm dummmm daaaaah.

"People change", says Rose.
"Oh, no they don't", says Ida. "Look at me. I've never changed. It's like those sticks of rock: bite it all the way down, you'll still read Brighton."

—

Meanwhile, Brighton is changing, but not as radically as it might.

Overlooking the sea, next to the neo-classical façade of Brunswick Terrace, a nineteenth century villa, Western House. Vesta used to live here.

It's

knocked down and replaced by

a miniature golf course

and then

Embassy Court, a block of flats designed by the architect Welles
Coates in the modern movement style, a style ideally suited to
the seaside since all its buildings look like ocean liners—the De
La Warr Pavilion in Bexhill, the Grand Ocean Hotel in Saltdean,
Coates' Isokon building (misplaced!) in Hampstead. Embassy
Court has a rectilinear cross-section for nine storeys, each with
a cantilevered balcony, and then tapers asymmetrically for two
storeys at the top. If the tapering were to continue on up, the
building would float away. (An amphibious building! When the
residents need a holiday in France, all they have to do is agree,
and off it goes to Dieppe.)

State-of-the-art luxury! Space heating, thermal energy storage,
a bank on the ground floor, penthouse suites, a bar. "Old ideas
have been discarded", says Coates, "and a new building has
arisen to greet a new age that thinks of happiness in terms of
health." Alderman Sir Herbert Carden is so excited by Embassy
Court that he campaigns for every other building along the
seafront, from Hove to Kemp Town, to be demolished and
replaced by something like it.

The Regency Society is formed, rapidly. The seafront strip
survives.

—

And Brighton creeps eastwards along the cliffs towards
Newhaven—Woodingdean, Ovingdean, Rottingdean, Saltdean,
Telscombe Cliffs, Peacehaven—suburbs, villages, villages that
become suburbs.

I set off east on the Undercliff walk. Chalk, flint, concrete,

granite, chalk, water. To my left are the cliffs; in front of me
a pedestrian walkway (a super-highway!) on the top of the
seawall; to my right the sea.

It's high tide. Waves smash against the sea wall, and over it.
Children scream with delight.

It's low tide. Kilometre after kilometre of rock covered with
black seaweed. What if it were edible?

It's high tide. Water laps into the sea wall.

It's low tide. Birds congregate on the rocks. Water licks at the
rocks playfully, experimentally, like a dog.

The birds swoop, glide, hover in front of the cliffs. On a sunny
day, their shadows follow them. No they don't. They behave
much more unpredictably, slowing, racing, distorting, disap-
pearing, depending on the exact contours of the cliff face. It's
like the relationship between twin sisters, one honest, reliable,
slightly goody-two-shoes, the other playful, naughty, subversive.

What is that growing on the cliffs? (And how can it possibly
grow there?) That must be valerian, that's definitely sea kale.
Is that deadly nightshade?

Ovingdean. Ferocious beach huts that look like a relic of
communism. At the top of the cliff, a home for blind veterans
with a spectacular view. And behind it the suburban expansion
of a thirteenth-century village.

And on towards Rottingdean. Bands of flint run across the cliff.
Some are diagonal but most are almost perfectly horizontal.
Here and there a flint protrudes. This strange sealandscape
is described in a strange book *Thoughts on a Pebble* by Gideon
Mantell—short, discursive, full of illustrations, quotations,
poems—a minute discussion of how a flint comes into existence.

In 1822 Mantell, obstetrician and palaeontologist, looks
at a gigantic tooth his wife Mary has found in a quarry in
mid-Sussex and realises that it is the tooth of a prehistoric

reptile, which he calls the Iguanodon. The discovery is met with scepticism: the poor man has got his dates muddled | he's only a country doctor | it was some kind of rhino | it was some kind of fish; but it is, finally, accepted by the Royal Society—a unique moment of exhilaration in a life plagued by self-doubt. In 1833 the Mantells move to Brighton. He announces that his palaeontology will not get in the way of his medical practice, but his patients don't believe him. The practice fails. The Town Council offers to turn his house into a museum of fossils. The museum fails because of his habit of waiving the entrance fee. Mary leaves him, taking their four children. He sells his collection to the British Museum. He falls into a series of unwinnable palaeontological spats with Richard Owen, Hunterian professor at the Royal College of Surgeons, "overpaid, overpraised, and cursed with a jealous monopolising spirit". Owen has classified the three pre-historic reptile species which have been discovered—megalosaurus, iguanodon and hylaeosaurus—as dinosaurs, a word he has coined ("terrible lizards"). A creationist, he argues that dinosaurs were "God's monsters", and infuriatingly claims to have discovered the iguanodon. Mantell injures his spine in a carriage accident, and is in constant pain. He dies of an accidental overdose of opium. His spine is exhibited in Owen's museum—posthumous insult—to exhibit "the severest degree of deformity".

In *Thoughts on a Pebble*, Mantell describes the chalk cliff (pre-seawall) extending into the Channel, "probably to the opposite coast of France". The beach was once "formed of chalk-flints, that at some remote period were detached from their parent rock, and broken, rolled, and thrown together, by the action of the waves. We are certain of this because we know that flints cannot grow; that they were originally formed in the hollows or fissures of other stones; and upon inspecting" any of the flints "more attentively, we perceive, not only that such was the case, but also that it has been moulded in *Chalk*, for it contains the remains of certain species of extinct shells and corals, which are found exclusively in that rock. Here then a remarkable phenomenon presents itself for our consideration:

this flint, now so hard and unyielding, must once have been in a soft or fluid state, for the delicate markings of the case and spine of an *Echinus*, or Sea-Urchin, are deeply impressed on its surface... and there are here and there portions of minute corals, and scales of fishes..."

—

My father teaches physics for forty years and then starts making sculptures out of flints, an idea that has preoccupied him for most of his working life. Friends and relatives are co-opted to drive him up to the Downs to collect material. He looks at a flint and sees a head, an arm, a torso, a foot, a penis. The flints are assembled in my parents' garden in categories. Yes, it's creepy—sometimes you remember they're just flints, sometimes you forget. He sticks the flints together to make human figures—contemplative men, gymnastic women, dancing couples. Some are monumental, made from huge flints; some are small, light, delicate. They are at the same time newly minted and primeval.

Then comes a phone call; he has an exhibition. We are pleased for him, and full of dread. We will help him pack up and transport the sculptures. It's a nightmare. They sit awkwardly on wooden paletts, surrounded by bubble wrap, held in place with sticky tape. But they're fragile, and they have a terrible tendency to collapse into their constituent flints in transit. So the days before each exhibition are a race to reconstruct.

During one of these reconstruction races, at Firle Place, near Lewes, there is a further problem. My father arrives on the morning of the exhibition opening to find that all the penises have been removed from the sculptures. He hunts down the owner of the house, the primeval Lord Gage, in his study, and tells him of the loss. "I have them here", says Lord Gage, opening a drawer of his desk. "We simply can't have them on display. They are disgusting and offensive." My father patiently explains that the sculptures are inspired by ancient Greek and Roman statuary, and that the penises are essential. Lord Gage reluctantly hands them over, and my father dashes around in his best three-piece tweed suit sticking them back into place.

—

Rottingdean. A gap in the cliffs, and the village sweeps up from the beach, a genteel antidote to bad Brighton. Rudyard Kipling was here. All is well, just so.

And on to Saltdean, dominated by the confident modernism of the Art Deco Lido and the Grand Ocean Hotel (now the grand ocean block of flats). The pedestrian super-highway opens out into a giant super-bowl—a space that should surely host a continuous rock festival—and comes to an end. Beyond it, the cliffs have to fend for themselves.

—

On the way back, past Ovingdean, a military-looking door leads into the cliff. The door to Roedean. There is a notice on it, a heart-breaking appeal for sightings of a lost teenager. Through the door a tunnel leads up to the school, a school for girls only.
"Honour the worthy and honour the keen", the girls sing, "Honour her daughters, and honour Roedean."
This building was built to look terrifying—terrifying to the girls, to the teachers, to visitors, to bad boys from Brighton College trying to force entry. Recently the school had an influx of Chinese pupils, their parents seduced by its Englishness. Put off by the influx, English parents looked elsewhere. Put off by the lack of Englishness, Chinese parents looked elsewhere. Through the tunnel, past the Head Mistress's study, across the lacrosse pitches, over the fence, up Happy Valley and we're in Woodingdean, once rolling hills overlooking the sea, populated exclusively by sheep and horses. After the First World War, the landscape takes a different shape. Plots are sold for development, often to former soldiers. A glorious act of generosity | a cynical act of exploitation. The first dwellings are shacks, wooden huts, railway carriages.

—

Lij Tafari Makonnen.

One of the missions of the Rastafari is to establish a kingdom of God for black people. In 1927 Marcus Garvey, Black Nationalist, says: "Look to Africa, where a black king shall be crowned. He shall be your saviour." Three years later, Ras Tafari Makonnen is crowned Emperor of Ethiopia.

He is Haile Selassie, King of Kings, Lord of Lords, Conquering Lion of the Tribe of Judah. He is King Alpha and Queen Omega. He is HIM (His Imperial Majesty). He is Jah, he is Jah Jah, he is Jah Rastafari. He is Elect of Himself.

He becomes a messiah for the Rastafari, the second coming. Ethiopia is their Promised Land, their Zion.

"I am a man", he says. "I am mortal. I will be replaced by the coming generation. Don't make the mistake of thinking, don't make the mistake of pretending that a human being can emanate from a deity."

But the Rastafari take no notice.

In 1935, in an attempt to build an Italian empire, Mussolini's Fascist regime attacks Ethiopia. HIM speaks to his people: "If you refuse to resist our enemy who is coming from a distant country to attack us, if you persist in not shedding your blood, you will be rebuked by your Creator and cursed by your offspring."

Despite this rhetoric, the Italians have a massively superior army, and the Ethiopians are defeated. HIM is exiled. He makes an impassioned speech, in his native Amharic, to the League of Nations, begging for help in resisting the Fascists. The League futz around, impose a few sanctions and try to pretend the problem has gone away.

HIM comes to Britain. Hilda and Richard Seligman, recently arrived from Poland, refugees from Fascism, offer him a home. Hilda, a talented amateur sculptor, creates a wooden bust of his head. He travels with his family and a retinue. Bath, Swansea, Malvern. He spends holidays in a house in Woodingdean belonging to Max Miller, the Cheeky Chappie.

Max's variety act begins with the orchestra playing his signature tune, *Mary from the Dairy*. A spotlight appears on the curtain. Max waits at least ten seconds before appearing. He wears a floral suit with plus-fours, a kipper tie, a trilby hat and co-respondent shoes. He walks to the microphone and stands in his costume, silent, flirting with the audience. The laughter begins.

His material is risqué, full of double entendre. "When roses are red they're ready for plucking. When a girl is sixteen, she's ready for... 'Ere! I know exactly what you're saying, you wicked lot. You're the sort of people that get me a bad name." The act is punctuated with sentimental songs, comic songs.

Max and HIM are united in their hate for fascism and rationing. HIM can speak English fluently, but prefers French and Amharic, so their conversations are mediated by a translator.

"We have set out", says HIM, "to the best of Our ability to improve internal administration by introducing into the country western modes of civilisation through which Our people may attain a higher level. Hence Our conscience does not rebuke Us."

"Now there's a funny thing", says Max. His jokes are lost in translation.

In late September, early one evening, they walk together into the nearby valley. At the bottom is a hamlet: a manor house, a cricket ground, a couple of farms, an orchard, a few cottages, a Norman chapel. The buildings are abandoned, derelict, full of holes. The residents have been cleared out, and the place is being used for target practice. A light aircraft, a Cessna, stands next to the chapel.

But Max and HIM haven't come to witness target practice, which is finished for the day anyway. They have come with a mission. They pick plums from the orchard, vast quantities of plums, unrationed plums, and take them back to The Grange. The plums are made into jam, into a pie, into a pickle.

In 1941, when the Allies reclaim Ethiopia, HIM is reinstated as Emperor, to the great joy of his people.

After the Second World War Woodingdean grows, becomes itself, its suburban self. The Sunblest factory arrives, which does for bread what Woodingdean is doing for the countryside. The Grange is knocked down and replaced by a row of bungalows.

In 1957 Hilda's bust of HIM is mounted on a plinth and displayed in the park near her house. HIM comes over from Ethiopia for the ceremony. There is a photograph of him shaking Hilda's grandson's hand, very solemnly, as if the boy were a dignitary.

The bust sits in the park. No one takes much notice of it. To most people it has no meaning. Even if they stop to look at the plaque, they probably have no interest in an Emperor of Ethopia. Except. Rastafari come from all over the city, all over the country to pay homage. There is a three-day festival, a grounding, every year.

To begin with, Hilda is bewildered by the Rastafari, but she comes to accept them, then to love them. She is enchanted by their cheerful slowness, and, coming from an immigrant family herself, sympathises with them as outsiders. And the Rastas love her. She appears at their festivals, where she is hauled up onstage, introduced to the audience, made a fuss of. She is even invited to sing. (She refuses.)

Television becomes more and more popular. Max's work evaporates. He says: "When I'm dead and gone, the game's finished." He dies in 1963. The playwright John Osborne writes in his autobiography: "Max was a God, a saloon-bar Priapus."

HIM speaks to the United Nations. "Until the philosophy which holds one race superior and another inferior is finally and permanently discredited and abandoned", he says, "everywhere there's war. And until the basic human rights are equally guaranteed to all without regard to race—it's war. And until there's no longer first-class or second-class citizens of any nation, until the colour of a man's skin is of no more significance than the colour of his eyes—it's war."

In Ethiopia, political dissidents are imprisoned and tortured. Students protest. Famine takes hold in the north-east. A brutal civil war with Eritrean separatists. HIM's popularity begins to crumble. In 1974, after a coup d'état led by the Ethiopian army, he is imprisoned. He continues to believe that he is still Emperor. A year later, he dies in prison. Is he murdered? Probably not. Allowed to die by his captors? Possibly. Is his death faked? Definitely, according to the Rastafari. He is still their messiah. No corpse has been produced, they say. He is living under a new name: Abba Keddus.

In 1992 HIS body is found buried under a lavatory in the royal palace in Addis Ababa.

In 2020 the Oromo singer Hachalu Hundessa, fierce critic of the Ethiopian regime, is shot dead. Later that week, Hilda's statue of HIM in Cannizaro Park is taken down, hacked to pieces by Oromo protesters. The statue of Max Miller in Pavilion Gardens stands proud, jaunty, beyond backlash. There'll never be another!

—

1934
Oswald Mosley, devotee of Mussolini, holds a rally at the Dome. During his shape-shifting political career he has been a Conservative MP ("Germans have brought disease among us, reduced Englishman's wages, undersold English goods, and ruined social life"), an Independent MP, a Labour MP ("The banking system must be nationalised; there must be a minimum wage"). With other disgruntled members of the

Labour Party, including his first wife Cimmie, he has formed the New Party and then immediately hauled it in the direction of fascism. (Cimmie is appalled.) He has urged the formation of a vigilante group of young men to provide protection for the party's political meetings. This reminds us of the Nazi party, say his colleagues. "The only methods we shall employ shall be English ones", says Mosley. "We shall rely on the good old British fist." He abandons the New Party to form the British Union of Fascists (BUF). "The great Italian represents the first emergence of the modern man to power." The BUF is anti-globalisation, anti-Semite, anti-democracy, argues for a Corporate State—the government overseeing corporations formed of employers, trade unions and consumer interests— an end to the party system.

An audience of men, men, many men in black shirts. ("The black shirt is the outward and visible sign of an inward and spiritual grace.")

"Fascism", says Mosley, "above all rests on teamwork, the ability to pull together, the power to subordinate every interest of section or individual to the nation as a whole." On the Dome stage he is like a panther. He postures, grimaces, switches on and off his gleaming teeth. The men in black shirts are transfixed. The sound of communal singing sneaks into the auditorium. The men in black shirts are confused. "England is not finished, England is not dead", says Mosley. "I ask you to lift up your voices, to send to all the world a message: England lives, and marches on." At this moment he understands that he is being drowned out by a rousing rendition of *La Marseillaise*, which comes from the great chandelier under the dome. Guerilla music. Two days before, with the aid of Harry Cowley, anti-fascist chimney-sweep, workers disguised in painters' overalls have installed a speaker in the chandelier, connected it by a cable through the skylight of the Dome, over the roof, across the street through a tree, and into the office of the Labour councillor Lewis Cohen. The rest of the meeting is chaos. In the tree, a bullfinch sings *La Marseillaise*.

A few years later the blackshirts, marching down the Walworth Road in London, singing the *Horst Wessel Lied*, are met by a group of communists (and a bullfinch) singing *The Red Flag*. But all of them—blackshirts + communists + bullfinch— are drowned out by the local inhabitants singing *Rule Britannia* and *Land of Hope and Glory*.

—

## 1940

Early-warning radar stations are reporting echoes out at sea. Are they ships? Are they aircraft? Air raid warnings are activated. Nothing there. There's nothing there. The operators call them angels. Lines of angels move along the coast, and the lines of angels are starlings. What the operators have detected are the reflections of moving wings.

Down below, on the beach, barbed wire fencing and concrete barriers. If there is an invasion, the plan is to destroy the Palace Pier and the West Pier to prevent the Germans using them as landing stages. Brighton, too near France, is a dangerous place to be. Hope and glory.

Defence Regulation 18B allows the Home Secretary to imprison without trial anyone he believes might "endanger the safety of the realm". Mosley is imprisoned, with his second wife Diana Mitford. (They have married in secret, in the drawing room of Joseph Goebbels' house, Adolf Hitler one of the six guests.) Winston Churchill grants permission for the Mosleys to live in a small house inside Holloway Prison, with a garden where they may sunbathe and grow vegetables, and to employ fellow prisoners as servants.

—

## 1948

The BUF has been dissolved. The Fascist movement is in retreat, but Mosley is not. He has a new vehicle for a new idea: the Union Movement. He argues for British integration into Europe and an end to immigration from the commonwealth. "We can live in peace and friendship", he says, "side by side, in separate nations and separate developments. But we cannot have the mix-up of peoples and races who are widely different and divergent. It will lead to nothing but trouble." The many men of the Union Movement march through Brighton. At the Level (an open space which has been used (on Boy George's instruction) as a cricket ground, for celebratory public banquets, for sex work, for political meetings, and will be used for a peace camp, for a skate park, for drug deals) they are beaten up by a group of elderly Jewish men armed with walking sticks and umbrellas.

Britain, reluctantly, relinquishes its empire, becomes poorer, and, reluctantly, begins to integrate into Europe.

—

When does Brighton become committedly, consciously, conspicuously queer? A queer haven, a queer magnet.

Gay men and lesbians come to live in Brighton, come down from London for the weekend. Are they welcome? There are sympathetic landlords. There are sympathetic pubs, clubs, bars: Pigotts, The Greyhound, The 42, The Curtain, The Queen of Clubs, The Lorelei, The Spotted Dog.

But the police are not sympathetic. The clubs are raided randomly, regularly. (Homosexuality is illegal. But dancing and drinking coffee are not. And lesbianism is beyond the law. The lawmakers don't see it as a problem | can't quite believe it exists.)

There are high-status gay men—the acceptable face of homosexuality—who are invulnerable to these attacks. For one thing these men would never be seen dead in any of the clubs. For another, they are coy about their homosexuality. There are partners, there are lovers, but they are kept hidden away. Many of these men work in the theatre: Robin Maugham, novelist, playwright, viscount; Terence Rattigan, playwright, knight of the realm; Douglas Byng, pantomime dame, "the high priest of camp."

There are high-status lesbians. "Nothing was worse than the theatrical lezzies of that period", says Kay, a non-theatrical lezzie. "They were even more superficial than anyone. They quarrelled all the time, they drank too much. They were all refined and ladylike, as it were, and then suddenly you'd realise they'd just had too many gins, so they'd start on each other: snip snip snip snip." (There is war on the culture, and there is civil war.)

And there is Dusty. "Many people say I'm bent", says Dusty, "and I've heard it so many times that I've almost learned to accept it... I know I'm perfectly as capable of being swayed by a girl as by a boy. More and more people feel that way and I don't see why I shouldn't."
"You should", says Kay. "You should."

Some of the clubs are short-lived, some renounce their queer support, but generally there is a mood of defiance. Kemp Town becomes the centre of gay life. This is where Piers and Jamie and I are brought up, and we haven't a clue what's going on. (Jamie has always admitted that his gaydar is no good.)

—

Dusty helps to make black music white. Her style: blue-eyed soul, rooted in gospel. Her voice is breathy, sensual, at once powerful and vulnerable. Just call me angel of the morning.
"You don't own me", she sings,
"I'm not just one of your many toys.
You don't own me,
Don't say I can't go with other boys."
And don't say I can't go with other girls.

"People say I'm gay, gay, gay, gay, gay, gay, gay, gay", says Dusty. "I'm not anything. I'm just... People are people... I go from men to women. I don't give a shit."

—

In 1964 there is an idea: the Skydeck. A tower out at sea, 1000 feet high, linked to the seafront by a new pier. At 600 feet, three observation decks, fitted out like an ocean liner, bars, a nursery and a pool with porpoises and dolphins. Lifts to take you up and down. Brighton as it could have been. (Actually, Brighton as it now is, in a watered-down version: the i360.)

—

Then there's another idea: Biba. This one happens.

Barbara Hulanicki comes to Brighton in 1948. The UN has just partitioned Palestine. Her father Witold, the Polish Consul General, a mediator between the Jewish and Arab states, is assassinated in Jerusalem by the extreme Zionist group the Stern Gang. Hulanicki lives with her Aunt Sophie, studies at Brighton Art School, becomes a fashion illustrator, realises that no one is making the clothes she would like to wear, designs a pink gingham dress, size 8 only, wins a competition, opens a shop Biba (her sister's name) at 21 Queen's Road: mini-skirts, frocks, floppy felt hats, feather boas, velvet trouser suits, tee shirts in mulberry, plum, green, chocolate-brown lipstick. Who are these clothes for? "She is pretty and young. She has an upturned nose, rosy cheeks, and a skinny body with long asparagus legs and tiny feet." It turns out there are plenty of people answering this description. Biba and Mary Quant define British fashion. Ten years later Biba has taken over the department store Derry and Toms in London, given it an Art Deco makeover, installed a million mirrors, a food hall in which all the produce has black labels, a Rainbow Room, penguins. Short-lived. "People would walk out of the shop with stuff and the girls couldn't care less." At the closing down auction, Piers buys the entire knitwear counter for peanuts; he is competing with a random raggle-taggle crowd of hippies and freaks.

—

Spiv and Pat come to our AirBnB for Mod Weekend. They bring several suitcases full of clothes, ready to get into character— psych-Mod, punk-Mod, metal-Mod, freakbeat-Mod, Ska mod.

In the 1950s being a Mod is about modern jazz, art films, coffee bars. Beatnik culture. In the 1960s being a Mod morphs.

A sharp suit, a parka, a Lambretta with a massive bank of mirrors and headlights, amphetamines, clubbing. The Kinks, the Small Faces—R'n'B with lurking music hall, Otis Redding in a special relationship with Max Miller.

Meanwhile Teddy Boys, in fancy waistcoats, long jackets, tapered trousers, brothel creepers, armed with iron bars, butchers' knives, weighted leather belts, are morphing into Rockers. For a Rocker, a heavyweight motorbike, leathers, metal studs, no helmet. The danger must be conspicuous. It's a straightforwardly macho thing, and to a Rocker a Mod is a sissy, an effeminate freak, at home in effeminate Brighton. Originally Gene Vincent, Eddie Cochrane, now The Rolling Stones, The Pretty Things. Rock'n'roll with the rumblings of heavy metal.

Culture wars! The Mods and the Rockers come to Brighton for mutual provocation. Chalk and cheese. No, chalk and soot. The Mods are given chalk and the Rockers soot, and they are encouraged to attack each other, playfully. (Have I invented this?) Real violence lurks. The Whitsun weekend in 1964 is chaos: the two tribes running, running, jumping from the promenade, clashing with each other, police everywhere. How violent is this violence? It's a battle of deckchairs. But the media goes on the rampage.

The weekend is mythologised on film:

Quadrophrenia.

The two lovers, Mods, running from the police, fall through a doorway into

a skuzzy twisty alleyway joining East Street to Little East Street

and have sex there:

Jimmy and Steph.

Piers comes home with two singles (oh what was a single? a single was a double, two songs, one on either side of a small vinyl disc—oh you knew?) that change my view of what is to come. I'm fourteen years old. *Itchycoo Park* by the Small Faces and *We Love You* by The Rolling Stones. They terrify me and they excite me. They make me long to stay a child and long to become an adult. *Itchycoo Park* (where's that?) with its strange verses:
"I feel inclined to blow my mind,
Get hung up, feed the ducks with a bun",
its subversive middle eight:
"You can miss out school—won't that be cool?
Why go to learn the words of fools?"
and its jaunty chorus:
"It's all too beautiful
It's all too beautiful."
Oh, the flanged drum sound! Is this what drugs sound like?
The Small Faces have gone psych.
*We Love You* with its crash-of-prison-door-closing opening.
Mick Jagger and Keith Richards have been arrested for possession of drugs. They have become pariahs and heroes. This is their response.
"You will never win we
Your uniforms don't fit we
We love you, we love you, and we hope
That you will love we too."
Eerie falsetto voices, mellotron. Is this what drugs sound like?
The Rolling Stones have gone psych.

In the mid-1970s being a Mod morphs again. Skin-mod, punk-mod. It has become almost the opposite of its original form. In the 1980s Ska, 2-Tone. After that it's all revival.

Spiv and Pat, fiction-tourists, go to pay homage to Jimmy and Steph in Quadrophenia Alley. The walls are covered with mirrors, and vinyl, and names, and messages: "Love is everywhere, the rest is dust", "Cum in my mouth." They add their names, and drop into Quadrophenia Alley the shop to buy some more Mod clothes.

Ann Quin, born in Brighton of a working mother and an absentee father, dies in Brighton when she walks into the sea by the Palace Pier and never returns. Stones in her pockets? Like Virginia Woolf, she has had a turbulent mental life punctuated by breakdowns. She has written four experimental novels: *Berg*, *Three*, *Passages*, *Tripticks*. Berg introduces Brighton fictional scumbag no.3. "A man called Berg, who changed his name to Greb, came to a seaside town intending to kill his father." Berg | Greb is a hair tonic and wig salesman, a man who would certainly have advertised in the *Brighton Patriot*. "BUY BERG'S BEST HAIR TONIC DEFEAT DELILAH'S DAMAGE: IN TWO MONTHS YOU WILL BE A NEW MAN." He stalks his absentee father Nathaniel, an amateur ventriloquist, and his father's mistress Judith, who live in a claustrophobic boarding house "reminiscent of an Egyptian tomb", full of antiques and stuffed animals. He listens to them having sex. Dressing as Judith ("the nylons against his legs gave him an almost erotic pleasure"), he narrowly avoids being raped by his drunk father. He wants sex with Judith, and he doesn't want it. Does he want any kind of relationship? He vacillates, procrastinates, considers suicide, flounders in a sea of paranoia. "Defeat the desire and act", he thinks. He does commit a murder, but the victim turns out to be his father's ventriloquist's dummy.

*Berg* is written from Berg | Greb's viewpoint, a shape-shifting, macabre, dirty, vaudevillean monologue, Virginia Woolf in cahoots with Patrick Hamilton and Max Miller. Brighton, out of season, is empty, claustrophobic, bleak. "The huddled shapes of tramps moulded into their lumps of rags and newspaper, twitching and squirming under the pier", spent balloons and used contraceptives dividing pavement from road, men masturbating in grimy cinemas, smells of alcohol and stale tobacco, of seaweed, oil and tar.

—

The Brighton of *The West Pier*, of *Brighton Rock*, of *Berg*, this fictional Brighton, which can't be entirely fictional or it wouldn't have found its way into fiction, is a place which manufactures disappointment.

—

Dusty sings *Wishin' and Hopin'*. The Sexual Offences Act legalises homosexuality, partially, partially. Private homosexuality is allowed. Public homosexuality carries an increased penalty. At The Spotted Dog there is cautious jubilation. "There is no occasion for jubilation", says Lord Arran, co-sponsor of the bill. "Any form of ostentatious behaviour, now or in the future, any form of public flaunting, would be utterly distasteful and would, I believe, make the sponsors of this bill regret that they have done what they have done."

—

As Dusty sings *In The Land Of Make Believe* there's another idea: the Marina.

This isn't a new idea. The first scheme, put forward in 1806, was for two stone piers, stretching out from the ends of West Street and East Street eight hundred feet into the sea and curving inwards, to accommodate two hundred ships. Brighton as it might have been.

"No one who has the good fortune to live in Brighton", says the poet John Betjeman, "will think that a garish pleasure slum built on the water will benefit the town." The Marina that is built at Black Rock is not so much a garish pleasure slum as a concrete monument, a monument to concrete: a monumental concrete seawall with a monumental concrete motorway leading down to it. Oh yes and there's some Lego housing with names like Sovereign Court and Victory Mews, bestowed by budding Brexit enthusiasts, a casino and a branch of Asda, which has the word George emblazoned on it. (A tribute to Boy George? Or Loyal George? Probably not.) This is not Brighton—it's a suburb of Brighton with sailing boats.

—

Richard Stilgoe (Sir Richard Stilgoe!) is standing by his Rolls Royce. He has collaborated successfully with Andrew Lloyd Webber, my least favourite composer, and now he is collaborating with me. He has come to see me for a meeting, and he has phoned me to say he is outside my house, but he is not outside my house. There has been a mild GPS malfunction. I walk round the corner into Little Preston Street to retrieve him. He and his shiny car are outside the brothel, and so are a couple of middle-aged blokes in car coats. I am (mildly) miffed that he has mistaken a brothel for our house, but GPS evidence is hard to ignore. We get into his car and drive past a succession of chefs and waiters standing in the street smoking amongst the bins, because almost all the houses in Little Preston Street are kitchens, the kitchens of the restaurants in Preston Street. The smell is complex, confusing. Soon we're outside the house that houses Jo and me and is not a brothel. For some reason (vanity?) I'm expecting Richard to acknowledge the discrepancy, but he says nothing.

There is a house in Little Preston Street that is neither a restaurant kitchen nor a brothel: The Dependant—a (the!) perfect name for a pub, which is what it used to be, until it wasn't, until, until, until 1972, when it's unused, derelict, owned by a company which manufactures corkscrews (Made-in-Brighton update: typewriters, bubble cars, video games, skunk, corkscrews) and which hands over the keys to Richard Cupidi who opens the Public House Bookshop. Brave. In normal circumstances you'd probably never choose to walk into Little Preston Street, and you certainly wouldn't expect to find a book there. But here it is, this Victorian pub painted in salvaged caterpillar yellow enamel tractor paint. This is where you come for *Berg* and for queer books (it's a haven within a haven) and anarchist books and for *Brighton Voice*, worthy successor to the *Brighton Patriot*. "Don't wait around for the revolution to happen elsewhere", says *Brighton Voice*, "make the revolution happen in Brighton". This where you come if you want to meet Allen Ginsberg, or listen to free jazz, or prevent the Marina being built, or leave your baby (temporarily).

The shop is firebombed several times. The staff are given self-defence training. When a neo-Nazi group (is it the Racial Preservation Society, formed recently in Brighton?) threatens an attack, a volunteer group of anarchist bus drivers camps outside, and the attack is averted. A note written on a type-writer arrives: "A friendly warning… Because 'Brighton Voice' is a Communist front newspaper, shops which sell it have had their windows broken and other troubles. It is advisable therefore not to sell 'Brighton Voice' in your shop. 11th Hour Brigade." Has the 11th Hour Brigade learned their tactics from the suffragists? Probably not.

The shop survives, thrives, fails to prevent the Marina being built, and is finally killed off by Amazon. Richard Cupidi becomes a hypnotherapist.

—

The barriers are being erected. It's that time of year. Joe, key member of the group Momentum, the Faithfull-Wigney branch of the Labour party, comes to stay at our AirBnB. He wears a series of increasingly uncompromising Hawaiian shirts.

When it's not Blackpool, it's Bournemouth. When it's not Bournemouth it's Brighton. So clearly it must be by the seaside, and its name must begin with a B. (Bognor, Bexhill, Broadstairs, your time will come.) Why by the seaside? So that the delegates feel they're on holiday? But aren't they meant to be making important decisions about the future of the country?

The seafront is transformed. Kings Road becomes one lane so that the ring of steel can be put in place around the Brighton Centre, the ugliest building in the world. (But what a flexible space! Last week it was Squeeze, and the week before it was the Alpha Course.) The ring of steel is essential for status. For a Lib Dem conference it is noticeably absent. The austerity of the ring of steel is mildly mitigated by a carpet of Astroturf and some potted plants. Security guards lurk in doorways.

And you could argue that this is entirely necessary. In 1984 the Tories are here, the lady with the handbag and voice training with her faithful acolytes. (Brighton has recently voted overwhelmingly in her favour. Is this what I fought for? thinks Clementina Black.) The miners' strike is six months in. Thatcher has been referring to their leaders as "the enemy within". She and her cabinet, her cohort of blokes, are staying at the Grand Hotel. Gummer, Tebbit, Howe. (This was the hotel at which my grandparents used to stay when they came for a holiday here; my mother and her sisters would stay at a BnB with the nanny, occasionally meeting up with their parents for an affectionate few minutes on the promenade.) Almost a month before, Patrick Magee of the Provisional IRA has stayed in the hotel under the pseudonym Roy Walsh. He has planted a time bomb, wrapped in cling film to fool the sniffer dogs, he has checked out, and he is waiting for the entire cabinet to be destroyed. He is a disappointed man; five people are killed, but none of them are cabinet ministers. Thirty people are injured. He has planted the bomb in the wrong part of the hotel.

The next day, the Provisional IRA vows to try again. Mrs Thatcher, its statement reads, will now realise that Britain cannot occupy our country and torture our prisoners and shoot our people in their own streets and get away with it. Today we were unlucky, but remember we only have to be lucky once. You will have to be lucky always. Give Ireland peace and there will be no more war.

The conference continues.
"The only sorrow of the Brighton bombing", says Morrissey,
"is that Thatcher escaped unscathed."
"The kind people" he sings,
"Have a wonderful dream,
Margaret on the guillotine.
Make it real,
Make the dream real."
(Thirty years later Morrissey is an ardent supporter of the extreme far-right party For Britain. "Britain", says Morrissey,

"is a negative place. It hammers you down and it pulls you back and it prevents you.")

The bombing gives Thatcher and her party a massive boost. Memories of World War Two. Terrorism triumphantly defied. Strong and resolute personal leadership.

Magee's fingerprint is on a registration card found in the wreckage. If that was my fingerprint, he says, I didn't put it there. He receives eight life sentences, but is released in 1999 under the terms of the Good Friday Agreement.

The Provisional IRA is disbanded. Jo Berry, the daughter of one of the victims, meets Magee, and a strange friendship rises up. "I don't like to use the word forgiveness", she says. "For me it is more about empathy and understanding." Together they become advocates for reconciliation.

—

Fifteen years after being gay is no longer illegal, AIDS has sneaked in, and to be gay is terrifying. Where did this invisible terror come from? How is it transmitted? Is it a death sentence? There is a tsunami of misinformation. The country is divided between sympathy and blame. Then a new law: Section 28. Local authorities and schools "shall not intentionally promote homosexuality." The enemy within. Homophobia rises. The country veers towards blame and disgust. The response in Brighton is a wave of activism and protest, the start of the Brighton Pride Festival, and a defiant explosion of gay culture.

—

In Brighton you can dance. Bharatanatyam, Break Dance, Dubstep, Kabuki. You can dance the waltz, the hand jive, the skronk, the paso doble, the allemande, the bachata, the tango, the bunny hop, the zapateado, the mule, the Harlem shake, the vogue, the krump, the Carolina shag. If you're not dancing on the bandstand, where there are ballroom dancing classes every Thursday evening, you're very likely to be dancing in a club underneath the arches on the seafront, so you can walk out of the door at any moment, listen to the sound of the waves and dance on the beach.

In 1986, the Zap Club, underneath an arch on the seafront, presents *Grotesque Dancer*. It's frisky, ironic, absurd. Conventional ideas of female beauty and sexuality are put through the mangle. Liz Aggiss is inspired by the work of Valeska Gert, subversive expressionist dancer of the 1920s. Male critics are baffled, disgusted. Female critics are sympathetic. "An eccentric mixture", writes the dance historian Marion Kant, "of offence and nonsense." At one moment, Liz Aggiss takes off her wig to reveal a shaven head. "Why do you have to make yourself so ugly?" shouts her father from the back of the club.

Later that night at the Zap Club it's Club Shame, "the blueprint for gay clubbing in the nineties".

—

First he is the bass player of The Housemartins, consummate pop act, with an ideology of Christianity and socialism. Take Jesus—Take Marx—Take Hope.

In 1988 Norman Cook comes to Brighton. He becomes Fatboy Slim. Brighton loves him. The city is revitalised.

He is Cheeky Boy, he is Stomping Pondfrogs, Margret Scratcher, Drunk Soul Brother, Pierre Burner Down, he is Yum Yum Head Food. He is Son of Cheeky Boy, he is The Feelgood Factor, Arthur Chubb, Biggie Slims.

2001 The Big Beach Boutique. A free concert on the beach. 35,000 people turn up. Glorious.

2002 The Big Beach Boutique 2. Norman underestimates his own popularity. 250,000 people turn up, jostling for space between the piers and on the promenade. People people people. People hang out of buildings, stand on cars, shin up to the top of lampposts. Some of the audience are so far away that they can't hear the music, let alone see. A flotilla of boats out at sea. An exquisite sunset. In the midst of the crowd, NORM-STOCK 2 on a massive Union Jack, LIFE IS A BEACH on a pennant. Norman, in and out of headphones, in and out, flirts with his audience like a modern Max Miller, lipsynching friskily to his own tunes. *Gangster Trippin'*. *Sunset (Bird of Prey)*. Behind him, a message comes up on the screen: HALLO FREAKS. The crowd is delighted to be described as freaks. The crowd is delighted. Pure euphoria. No one ever said it would be easy, dancing on pebbles. "Fatboy Slim is fucking in heaven", a voiceover raps. The crowd is fucking in heaven. This is how life should be.

Night begins to fall and the tide comes in and there is less space and there is no space and there are people people people, people are rescued unconscious from the sea, ferried off the beach by lifeboat because the streets are jammed and ambulances are inching through the crowds attempting to rescue the injured while people hang off the back of them, hoping to escape, but escape is not so easy because there's nowhere to go and the music goes on and there's nowhere and the music has to stop, stop now, you must all go home, and there is one train, just one train back to London and there are people people people, people wandering up the tracks, tumbling off the platforms while others jump into their cars and drive into the back of traffic jams which last for miles, and others give up trying to escape and sleep on the beach under the stars or under the Palace Pier.

The next day the media is on the rampage. A man has died of a heart attack in the middle of the tumult. (Yes, a man has died of a heart attack, but he was in a house.) A woman has lost her balance and fallen off the promenade—was she pushed? (Yes, a woman has fallen off the promenade, long after most people have gone home.)

I've created a monster, says Norman.

But Brighton still loves him.

—

Brighton Pride
(and no prejudice)
(a plea, a request, a demand, a call to arms)
(a celebration of queerness)
(a pink picnic)

becomes

a parade
(a reminder)
(where the streets have no shame)
(an opportunity to sell sex toys)
(the coast is queer)

becomes

a family day out
(a celebration of the (almost) acceptance of queerness)
(an opportunity for rainbow-washing)
(Britney Kylie Pet Shop Boys)
(*It's a it's a it's a sin*)

—

In Sheffield Jamie and Nick sing *People Will Say We're In Love*.

—

Heterosexual attraction—and repulsion—still exist in Brighton.
The cover of Helen Zahavi's *Dirty Weekend* features a crushed
stick of Brighton Rock. Inside, Bella, Brighton fictional scumbag
no.4 (is she a scumbag? is she really?) is being stalked, relentlessly (ah, Esther, ah, Rose). She visits a clairvoyant, Nimrod.
Tell me what frightens you, says Nimrod.
"Men frighten me. Their hunger frightens me. The way they
look at me frightens me. What I read in their eyes frightens
me."
Nimrod offers her a flick knife. (He has expanded his clairvoy-
ancy brand.)
Tell me what you want to be, says Nimrod.

"I want to be a spectator."

"You don't have that option."

"So I have no choice."

"You have a choice."

"What choice?"

"The only choice... Take the knife."

And she does. She turns stalker, and murderer. From victim to predator. From Esther to Gorse, from Rose to Pinkie. As she finishes off Jack, a serial killer, on the beach near the West Pier, she has a flash of understanding: "to stab him, she discovered, was to know him".

Brighton fictional scumbags nos.5–11: the seven stalkers whom Bella kills.

—

Who is Hoogstraaten? Hoogstraaten is a monster, a real-life scumbag, a slum landlord who despises his tenants, who despises women, who despises the world. He buys properties in Brighton with sitting tenants, bullies them, evicts them. When five people die in a fire in one of his flats in Hove, he describes them as "drug dealers, drug takers and queers—scum".

He pays a gang to throw a hand grenade into the Brighton house of Bernard Braunstein, a Jewish cantor. "I'm a Fascist", he says to Braunstein's wife Sylvia, "and a Nazi. If I wanted, I could pay £50 to men in London to get every Jew in Brighton bumped off." The judge describes him as "a sort of self-imagined devil who likes to think of himself as an emissary of Beelzebub."

In Brighton there is another scumbag landlord, Mohammed Raja. He and Hoogstraaten go into business together. Raja defaults on loans from Hoogstraaten. Hoogstraaten seizes some of Raja's properties. Raja sues Hoogstraaten for conspiracy and fraud. Raja is brutally murdered by two of Hoogstraaten's goons. Hoogstraaten is sentenced to ten years in prison, but is mysteriously acquitted on appeal.

He starts to build himself a mansion, and he calls it Hamilton

Place—no, HAMILTON PALACE. A palace intended to dwarf Buckingham Palace, with a monumental marble mausoleum. Thirty-five years later it is still unfinished. Someone suggests to Hoogstraaten that it be used to house the homeless. "The homeless", he says, "the majority of whom are so by their own volition or sheer laziness, are one of the filthiest burdens on the public purse today. The chance of my offering an opportunity to occupy my house is just ludicrous."

—

Embassy Court is now owned by cowboys. (Hoogstraten? No! Really? No!) It has fallen into disrepair. Keith Waterhouse has left, comparing it to an "East End slum". There is talk of demolishing it (and replacing it with a nineteenth century villa, no, perhaps not). The residents manage, after a long and acrimonious legal battle "more suited to a nursery school playground", to buy the freehold, and to renovate the building. Skint Records throw a party on the roof to celebrate. Anthony Seldon, the headmaster of Brighton College, puts it on his list of the ten best twentieth century buildings in Brighton, and simultaneously suggests knocking it down, along with "other excrescences on the seafront", and holding "a series of parties to celebrate".

—

It's a Wednesday, and Daniel and his friend Jez are off to Moulsecoomb, a sprawling hilly suburb of Brighton that struggles with poverty. Jez is hoping to be arrested. They are headed for the EDO MBM (ITT Integrated Structures) Technology Ltd factory again, to protest, as they have already protested, again and again, against the company's supplying of arms, or rather, components for arms, to the Israeli government, arguing that it is acting unlawfully by assisting war crimes in Gaza. (Made-in-Brighton update: typewriters, bubble cars, video games, skunk, corkscrews, arms components.) Smash EDO! Bombs out of Brighton! It's a weekly event. Marches, noise protests, blockades, lock-ins, roof occupations, art installations—and in response injunctions, prosecutions, helicopters, dogs, the imposition of an exclusion zone, the attempted banning of a campaign film (which, of course, promotes it), the infiltration of activist groups by an undercover police officer with a taste for strong lager and heavy metal. The confrontation is long-running, acrimonious, and occasionally pure pantomime. Last week a pink fibreglass car from a production of *The Wind in the Willows*, the driver in top hat and feathers, was used as a battering ram against police lines.

Brighton is a United Nations Peace Messenger City and the landlord of an arms factory. "We object to being called an arms factory", says Paul Hills, the managing director. "And we do not supply to Israel."

—

The Smash EDO Seven—Smith Saibene Woodhead Tadman Nicholls Osmond Levin are brought to trial. Smith Saibene Woodhead Tadman Nicholls have broken into the factory and sabotaged it by throwing computers and filing cabinets out of the windows. Osmond Levin have helped them. Criminal damage, says the prosecution. Citizens' decommissioning, says the defence. "I systematically destroyed what I could", says Ornella Saibene. "In my mind I saw images of the victims."

"You may well think", says the judge George Bathurst-Norman to the jury, "that hell on earth would not be an understatement of what the Gazans suffered in that time." The Seven are acquitted. The Zionist Federation calls for a mistrial. The judge has "behaved more like the defence counsel than the neutral officer he was meant to be". He is anti-semitic; he must be censured. No he is not he is simply upholding the law. He is anti-semitic! No! that is a grossly cynical attempt to undermine the significance of the acquittal. He is anti-semitic!!

Judge George is censured. The acquittal stands.

Ten years later, the EDO MBM (ITT Integrated Structures) Technology Ltd. factory in Moulsecoomb is still there. Smash EDO!

—

First there was Brighton and there was Hove.

Brighton: naughty, wrong, mildly dangerous, instilling fear, disgust, mild feelings of superiority in the citizens of Hove.

Hove: careful, right, mildly ashamed (or perhaps pretending to be ashamed), instilling mild feelings of superiority in the citizens of Brighton. Where do you live? Brighton, well, Hove actually. But that's ok isn't it? Brunswick Square is in Hove isn't it? That place where Stomp operates, that's in Hove isn't it? Fatboy lives in Hove, right? And the Brighton Centre is in Brighton, naff naff naff, and Churchill Square, and the Marina. Yes, yes, yes and yes, but is that enough?

Then the unification.
Brighton and Hove becomes BrightonandHove. A truce? A genuine rapprochement? Not really. It's more to do with the financial advantages of becoming a city.

And yet…

Peter Kyle Caroline Lucas Lloyd Russell-Moyle an openly gay man who fights against Brexit a woman the only Green MP in Britain who fights against Brexit an openly gay openly HIV-positive man who fights against Brexit—these three represent BrightonandHove. An oasis in a desert (or a desert in an oasis, depending on your viewpoint). The only non-Conservative MPs in the entire south-east of England. Spiritual descendants of Faithfull Wigney Carpenter. But the country is in the grips of the spiritual descendants (maybe the actual descendants?) of Sir Adolphus Dalrymple. Perhaps we need to detach ourselves from the rest of Britain and float out towards France. Amphibious city!

—

Nick Cave and Susie Bick come to Brighton, no no, to BrightonandHove.

Nick Cave writes a novel *The Death of Bunny Munro*, set in an unrevitalised Brighton, a coke-fuelled version of the Brighton in *The West Pier*, except that now the West Pier is derelict, and it's burning. Bunny Munro, child-man, man-child, Brighton fictional scumbag no.12, sells beauty products door-to-door (Bunny, meet Berg|Greb): "hands shit, face shit, body shit, hair shit". His wife has committed suicide. He goes on a sleazy, violent road trip around the city with his nine-year-old son. Booze, nicotine, drugs, endless attempts to get laid. The novel is in three parts: Cocksman, Salesman, Deadman.

Susie Bick is The Vampire's Wife, and that is a great success.

Nick Cave and Susie Bick's son Arthur, on an acid trip, falls off the cliff at Ovingdean. "There's just this thing", says Nick Cave, "and there's no way to navigate it. It just sits there and it fills up all the space. It fills up your body. You can feel it pressing against the insides of your fingers." He makes an album *Skeleton Tree*:
"You fell from the sky
Crash landed in a field...
You cried beneath the dripping trees
Ghost song lodged in the throat of a mermaid.
With my voice
I am calling you."
Then he makes an album *Ghosteen*.
"The stars are your eyes
I loved them right from the start
A world so beautiful
And I keep it in my heart."

Nick Cave and Susie Bick prepare to leave Brighton.
"It's become a more beautiful place to live, and a place where we can't live. It just resonates with meaning. But too much meaning."
They stay.

—

BrightonandHove as it could have been.

There is an idea: the King Alfred Leisure Centre, behind the beach in Hove, next door to Vesta and Clara's place, a slightly knackered massive brick bungalow (it has several storeys, but it's a bungalow) with swimming pool and ballroom, needs a makeover, no, that won't do, it needs replacing. There is a competition, with entries from the architects (the starchitects!) Richard Rogers, Wilkinson Eyre and, organised by my midwife brother Piers, Frank Gehry. Frank, the friskiest, the funkiest, the most famous architect in the world, has never had a building built in England. What an opportunity. In order to finance the leisure centre, there must be a million flats, or five hundred flats or something. Frank designs a dreamlike building which looks as if someone has put four crumpled multi-storey chef's hats on the beach. (Crinoline dresses! says Piers.) (Frank's signature: no straight lines.) The local residents are incensed. Frank wins the competition. The Dutch Bank ING promises money. The scheme shrinks in height and spreads, begins to lose its gorgeous irrational beauty. Frank comes to Brighton, looks alarmed, says to the council, If you want this building, you have to work with me. The council is split almost evenly between enthusiasm and distrust. The residents are still determinedly incensed. The scheme shrinks in height again. And is approved, by a whisker. Aaah, exciting, the most radical building in Brighton since the Pavilion. Boy George would approve. It will counterbalance the marina, draw tourists westward, make sense of BrightonandHove.

There is a global financial crash. ING withdraws. The end of the dream.

—

"Meat is murder", says Mary Shelley. The audience roars its approval, including the scattered omnivores who don't want to be identified by their silence.

We're in the kitchen of the Pavilion. It's the BrightonVegSlam. Tonight is the Battle of the Giants: Planet India versus Terre à Terre. Everyone is here: Gandhi of course Salt Zoella Carême Carpenter Caroline Lucas Gateau George Frank Gehry Dusty of course Sake Dean Mahomet Steve Ignorant Heather Mills our neighbour Natasha. Martha Gunn is the judge.

First up: Planet India, ft. Fatboy Slim. Confident Keralan crunk.

Powa Powa Powa
is what you get
if you take a slender
beautiful Basmati rice
grain and squash it
between the Bhagwat Gita
and the Ramayana
cook it with petit pois
coriander and spices
(not spicy, it's vegan, gluten free).
Powa Powa Powa
is what you get
No books were used
in the making of this dish

The audience is ecstatic. "Lovely", says Martha Gunn. "It would be good with roast chicken." The audience is outraged. "This is not a Poultry Slam", they shout. "Only joking", says Martha Gunn.

In the interval, Mary Shelley reads from her husband Percy's *A Vindication of Natural Diet*.

Now it's Terre à Terre, ft. Nick Cave. Bravely they slow the pace. Hypnotic Gagaku dubstep.

Dengaku
Aubergine Dengaku
Soft succulent baked aubergine,
drenched in white miso sweet ginger tahini marinade

topped with a black and white sesame seed crust and toasted sesame oil
served with a sesame ginger dressed salad of carrot and kohl rabi
with a smooth, tangy edamane, wasabi and yuzu pesto
finished with puffed rice wakame cracker shards
dusted with a hibiscus
amchur and nori salt

"Marvellous", says Martha Gunn. "Deep. Like being at the bottom of the sea." "Yes Martha", the audience shouts. "Good with baked mackerel!" "Very possibly", says Martha Gunn. "And complex too. More ingredients in that one dish than in my entire recipe book. What's amchur?"

She declares a dead heat. "There has to be a winner", says the audience. "Nonsense", says Martha Gunn, "competitions are for idiots. Shut up and eat."

—

Who is Zoella? What an idiotic question. Everyone knows who Zoella is. She determines the nation's tastes.

Bryony and her mother come to stay at our AirBnB. They are in Brighton because Bryony wants to be as close to Zoella, as close to Zoella-recommended products as she possibly can. Someone has posted a photograph of Zoella's front door (in Hove!) and Bryony and her mother are going off in search. Then shopping.

Difficult to search for Zoella. She's no longer a person—she's a brand. Shop the neon: a pair of lights in the shape of boobs, to remind you to check yours. Fifty festive manicure tips. Naked cakes bring the wow factor to any table. Enjoy next level masturbation. Do a digital detox.

Did you find the house? we say. No, says Bryony's mother, but Bryony loves Brighton. She wants to come and live here.

—

Gateau George, a.k.a. Le Gateau Chocolat, a.k.a. George
Ikediashi, born in Nigeria, a country which is pathologically
intolerant of gay people, comes to Britain, studies law. He takes
a job at NHS Direct. He is clinically depressed. He contemplates
suicide. Being a gay black man in Britain is easier than being
a gay black man in Nigeria, but it's not easy. He sits in a call
centre reading *Heat* magazine.

the child isn't his, he reads
her heartache
his mother speaks out

The phone rings.
"Hallo, NHS Direct, how can I help?...
yes, yes... yes, yes...
You got your ears pierced, that's nice...
yes, yes... yes, yes...
No, sir, it's unlikely that you have HIV. I really can't be sure
but..."
Enough. Call rejected.

cupcakes versus botox
a five-day detox
shellac your hair

Ring ring.
"Hallo, NHS Direct, how can I help?...
You took a taxi... The driver sped up over the bumps... Your
insides were all shaken...
No madam, it's unlikely... I expect you've still got your womb..."
Enough!! Call rejected.

No, no, no, no, no, thinks George, I've got a law degree! I can
sing! Get me out of here!

fairy-tale wedding
a honeymoon in paradise
five star resort

Ring ring ring. Call rejected. Job rejected.

So he does get out of there, and he comes to Brighton, because being a gay man in Brighton is easy and being a black man in Brighton is unusual but entirely possible, and this episode in the twilight zone becomes a song, for Gateau George is a singer with a luscious velvet baritone voice. I write the music. He performs it as part of an autobiographical cabaret *Black* at the Marlborough, a queer pub behind the Old Steine with a luscious velvet proscenium stage. Then he performs it in Edinburgh and Liverpool and London and the rest of the world.

"The most refreshing 'black' performer currently throwing down!" says Boy George, the other Boy George, Boy George 2, Culture Club Boy George. (I used to live next door to him in a squat in London. He borrowed our electricity.) "Period!" What do those inverted commas mean around the word *black*?

Gateau George, bearded, performs cabaret, dressed as a woman, singing Wagner, Gershwin, Nina Simone. He performs opera, dressed as a man, singing Wagner, Purcell, Kurt Weill. He plays himself, no, herself in Wagner's *Tannhauser* in Bayreuth. He is many selves.

"But you can't pass yourself off as a woman. You don't look like a woman", says Vesta. "You wear so much make-up, but you don't look like a proper woman. I'm not convinced, I'm not won over. You must wear the right underwear, you must focus on your deportment. And first of all, you must shave off that dreadful beard. Come round to St. Aubyn's Mansions. There's plenty of work to be done. I can help you."

"No you can't", says George.

—

Bob Dobbs is back!

At the 2019 general election (an election entirely dominated by Brexit) he is an independent candidate. The headshots

of the preppy man smoking his pipe appear on lampposts.
Encouraging tweets pour in:
"Love from the Dogtarian Cabal 111!
Howl, sniff, bark, shake.
The pipe will help us defeat you know who."
Bob, with 212 votes to Caroline Lucas's 33,151, fails to become
a MP.

—

Ali Smith, author of *How To Be Both*, about how to be both, introduces us in her novel *Summer* to Robert Greenlaw, man-child,
Brighton fictional scumbag no.74ish. (Brighton fictional scumbags nos.13–73ish can be found in the novels of Peter James
and Elly Griffiths. Man, man, man-child, man, child-man, man,
man…) Robert is an extremely intelligent thirteen-year-old
who uses his intelligence to battle with the world. Gorse, meet
Robert. Robert, meet Gorse. He takes the family Alexa down
to the beach hidden in his jacket and drops it casually over
the side of the Palace Pier into the sea shouting down after
it *Alexa, tell us how to do the breast stroke*. It is as if Robert has
attached a dimmer switch to his own brilliance, thinks his sister
Sacha, sixteen years old, extremely intelligent, fearful of the
state of the world. Her hero is Greta Thunberg, his is Dominic
Cummings, Brexit svengali (which in Ali-Smithworld makes
him, and Robert, class A scumbags). Robert flickers and flashes,
thinks Sacha, like one of the arcade machines on the pier.

Robert, choosing his theatre, the beach, superglues an egg-
timer to Sacha's hand, makes "a seagull claw, a birdsfoot, of her
hand." "From now on u always have time on ur hands", he texts
her. He has given himself a TOTAL HIGH. "The song he'd sing
if he could still sing would be about how time is more than
one thing, time is glass and sand, time is brittle and fluid, time
is fragile and tough, time is sharp and blunt, time is now and
ancient, time is before and after, time is smooth and rough and
if you try to remove your attachment to time, time will laugh
out loud and take the skin off you." For Robert, unlike the other
Brighton fictional scumbags, there is possible redemption. He
is fascinated by Einstein, and he is fascinated by Charlotte, a

stranger who helps Sacha deal with her birdsfoot. She is stunningly beautiful, he thinks. Her scent crosses Robert. She smells amazing. She is so clever it makes him feel weak.

Brighton in *Summer* has none of the menace it does in *Brighton Rock*. It is a city with a beach and a pier, a city where the Greenlaws are possible, Robert, Sacha, their mother Grace who used to be an actress and hasn't adjusted to not being an actress, their father who lives next door with a new partner. What Sacha loves about Brighton are the swifts. "The swifts came back!... They always come back to the same nesting place they left last year if they can, so long as it hasn't been renovated and made into an AirBnB—which no one except swifts can stay at now anyway because of the virus!"

—

There is no one staying at our AirBnB except swifts and seagulls. I am walking in the Lanes with Edie. There are no other human beings on the streets. Many of the shops are boarded up. The air-conditioning units are silent. Posters advertise events which never happened. Two foxes pad past, staring at Edie aggressively. Normally she would bark wildly and chase them, but here she is cowed. Look, you have deserted the place, say the foxes, don't be surprised that we're taking over. (But you were taking over anyway, before this, I think.) If you're searching for food, says Edie, you'll be disappointed. The seagulls have had whatever there is. It's a nightmare.

—

Indoor public space is out of bounds. Outdoor public space is a lifeline, the beach more than anywhere else. The beach is freedom. No swimming, no loitering, no sunbathing, but it's still freedom—common ground, not just a tourist magnet, a place to be reminded that the sky and the sea still exist, and that other human beings are not purely a digital fiction.

But you have to keep moving. The polite police are cruising. In the shelter of a groyne, a bunch of blokes has started a barbecue. "Put it out", say the polite police, several times.

"You're joking", say the blokes, several times. A policewoman takes off her helmet, walks into the sea, fills the helmet with water and pours it over the barbecue. "Move", she says.

—

"What are those things? Are they for torture?"
"Well... they're exercise machines."
"Why are they here on the grass?"
"It's a gym."
"It can't be a gym. Gyms are indoors. They're hidden away."
"Not any more they aren't."
"Look, that man is swinging a huge ball between his legs."
"It's doing him good."
"His face is very red. Is he going to explode?"
"I think he's hoping that next time his face will be less red."
"Can I have a go?"
"Er, no, it's only for grown-ups."
"Look, Flint is peeing on that mat. Oh look! Now he's peeing on that woman's rucksack."
"Oh fuck. Sorry sorry sorry, sorry. Sorry. Sorry."
"You said fuck!"
"Sorry, sorry. Fuck fuck fuck."

—

The empty hoardings at the top of our street, which were open invitations to Wartz and all, have been immaculately painted by an art collective.

After clapping the NHS and banging on saucepans and a massive gong which I might have been saving for this moment, we sing *Let It Be*, chaotically but with spirit. The next day, attached to the hoardings there is a message, embossed on tiny strips of metal, white capital letters on a luscious dark blue background. The blueness of the blue.
GAMMY
ART
GONGS AND LET IT
BE DOESNT CREATE
COMMUNITY

Culture war, albeit of the most delicate kind.
The war on Wartz is forgotten.

—

The sun is shining. Bad people are coming to Brighton. The police station themselves on the A23, next to a sign which reads The Rotary Club (Service above Self) welcomes you to Brighton, to intercept these immigrants. Brighton for Brightonians! You're absolutely right, says Donald Trump. Build a wall.

—

Edie and I set off up into Devil's Dyke. On the path is a line of people stretching up to the top of the dyke. It's like a pilgrimage. In lockdown there are two religions, the NHS and the natural world. Up here, inside the Downs, we are exploring our faith in the natural world, our attempt slightly compromised by our own presence.

We traipse past the only object in the dyke made by human beings, the only relic of Victorian Disneyland: a small concrete platform that was once one end of the cable railway. Today it's like an altar.

—

Angel House, the Georgian house next door to Embassy Court, is empty of people, but full of action, full of sound. Several kettles are whistling. On the radio in the guest bedroom, Barbara Hulanicki and Zoella discuss brand awareness, Hoogstraaten explains why his wives were his bitches. In the drawing room, a pianola plays a piece by Edward Carpenter. In the kitchen a magimix whirrs. Somewhere, a musical box plays *Abide With Me*. In the top bathroom buzzing electric toothbrushes stand on their chargers. There is a neat pile of clothes: Vesta's Burlington Bertie outfit, including the underwear. The shower is running. In the kitchen the timer goes off. The oven door springs open to reveal a perfect cheese soufflé (perfect for ten seconds!) made by Carême. A whispered conversation between Maria Fitzherbert and Esther Downes seems to come from under the floorboards. Angels in the architecture. The only living creature in the house is a bullfinch perched on the windowsill of the spare bedroom, singing Dusty's *Breakfast In Bed*.

—

I have a cough, so I am making a potion from the Martha Gunn Recipe Book. "Take coltsfoot and make a strong decoction of it till yr liquor is glutinous and sweetish of which you may drink as much as you can every day of what time you please." I drink as much as I can every day of what time I please, and soon I am well again.

—

Lockdown loosens a little. On the sea wall by the power station, next to "I really dislike paella", a new message appears: "Costa del bollocky". Below it, a Muslim couple frolics in the water. He wears red swimming trunks, she an enormous black dress, which billows chaotically out in the water. There is no question of swimming—who could wearing this dress?—but the two bob about cheerfully, flirtatious. (Where is Martha Gunn?) Their young children potter about on the beach, bored, disgruntled by the lack of attention, occasionally poking at an enormous barbecue that is dying down.

Next day the newspapers are on fire. Look at these photographs! Crowds of sun-worshippers! A major incident! Stay at home you craven Covid-carriers! Don't come down here from Derby!

—

Jo walks down Oriental Place, past the halfway houses, the hostels, the backpackers' hotels, towards the beach.
"Would you like an apple?" says Eddie.
"No thanks."
"What's your name?"
"Joanna."
"I love you Joanna."
"Yes, Eddie."

"But I'm not allowed to touch you."

"You're right Eddie."

"Would you like an apple?"

—

Lockdown loosens further. Everyone is confused. Most people want tighter restrictions. Meanwhile there is a protest march on the promenade. Save our rights! Say no to vaccines! Say no to the new normal! Say no to masks! Say no to tyranny! Covid is a lie! Bring a picnic, bring some music and let's have fun and say yes to life! The rest of the city looks on, bemused. Are these people from Brighton?

—

Edie and I walk through Palmeira Square at night (concentrate! Edie not Eddie). A woman on a bench in a hoodie and tartan trousers smokes a spliff. Edie disappears behind a bush, reappears. "I think she's found something to eat", says the woman. "It might be a mackerel." No, it's a face mask.

—

Lockdown again. Dusk, mid-winter. Since the Palace Pier closed the starlings have seized the opportunity and moved from the West Pier. An enthusiastic audience accumulates on the promenade. Apart from the odd set from a busker, it's the only live show in town. Everything else is on Netflix.

From further away, the murmuration looks like smoke. The pier is smouldering.

—

Thundering hooves. A stampede of horses, riderless, through the empty streets of Kemp Town.

—

There is a rumour that pets may be covid-carriers and will need to be vaccinated. A special vaccine centre will be set up at Black Rock. Dogs, cats, hamsters. Stick insects?

I am on the roof of our house. The gulls are everywhere. There are several nests, made of chicken bones, mussel shells, sticks, feathers, discarded face masks, plastic bags from Taj. Birds career past my ears, squawking, protecting their young. I lean out over the parapet and begin clearing the hopper. There is a thriving plant in there, some kind of weed I don't recognise, and underneath the remains of another nest. I potter around on the roof for a bit, picking up odd bits of slate and sticks. I begin to feel content, up above the city, in it but not in it, just me and the gulls.

I find myself spending more and more time up here, sitting on the parapet between our house and our neighbours', contemplating the sky, the city, the unusable i360. The gulls circle around me. It's as if they are teasing me, playing an elaborate game for my benefit. Occasionally I let out a tiny squawk, an experimental squawk: *huoh-huoh-huoh*.

—

The rewilding of the city has begun. Moles, rabbits, badgers, basking adders, beavers. Turtle doves, nightingales, purple emperor butterflies. Peregrine falcons hunt at night. What used to be shops are now permaculture farms: vegetables, fruit, herbs, skunk. Wolves roam the streets. The foxes are terrified.

—

Us

Them

Race

Horse

Swift

Chalk

# Water

Many many thanks to Corinne Pearlman, Shan Lancaster, Maureen Freely, Susannah Waters, Lennie Goodings, Jon Day, Sandy Nairne and Lisa Tickner, Jamie and Jessi Seaton, Jamie Muir for help and guidance; and to Sheila Rowbotham, The Brighton Mortiquarian, Victorian Commons, Unbound, Daring Hearts, The Keep, Emlyn Rees, Olivia Seligman, Luca Silvestrini and Schaun Tozer for wonderful source material.